The GHOST HUNTER'S FIELD GUIDE To CIVIL WAR BATTLEFIELDS

Fredericksburg & Chancellorsville

The Ghost Hunter's Field Guide To Civil War Battlefields

by
Mark Nesbitt

Author of
The Ghosts of Gettysburg
Series

Second Chance Publications

We have gathered the sacred dust,
of warriors tried and true,
who bore the flag of our nation's trust,
and fell in the cause
'tho lost, still just,
and died for me and you.

Confederate Cemetery
Spotsylvania, Virginia

Searchers after horror haunt strange, far places.

H. P. Lovecraft

TABLE OF CONTENTS

ACKNOWLEDGEMENTS

Many people have helped in the research and production of this book. I would like to thank the following:

Charlie Adams, III, Katie Butcher, Paul Chiles, Bob Coullier, Laine Crosby, Scott Crownover, Chris and Trista Couser from Eileen's at The Chimneys, Phyllis Erickson, Sheri Ferguson, The Fredericksburg Police Department, Rosemary Ellen Guiley, Jay Harrison, Karen Hedelt and the staff at the Fredericksburg Visitor Center, John Hennessy, the fine and knowledgeable staff at Kenmore, Craig Rupp, L. B. Taylor, The Kenmore Inn and staff, Julie Pellegrino, Pam Saylor, Russ Seymour, Smythe's Cottage, Tara and the staff at Claiborne's, Kris White from the National Park Service, The American Battlefield Ghost Hunter's Society, and my editor, wife, and favorite companion on my journeys, Carol Nesbitt.

INTRODUCTION

My first trip to the Civil War battlefields around Fredericksburg, Virginia, was in my teens. I was, at that age, a bona fide Civil War "buff." My formative early teenage years (1961–1965) were, coincidentally, the centennial of the most divisive war this country had ever known. At that time, information on the "War Between the States" was ubiquitous, from "Life" Magazine articles, to television specials on Mathew Brady's photography, to television series like "The Americans," set in Harper's Ferry, scene of John Brown's aborted raid to emancipate the slaves. I begged my father to take me to Gettysburg during the 1963, One-hundredth Anniversary, reenactment of the battle. He turned me down, reasoning it would be overwhelmed with tourists. (I later learned, after living in Gettysburg and asking some locals who had participated in the Centennial Celebration, the town was practically deserted. Everyone, apparently, had reasoned the same way my father had.) National Geographic had a special edition chronicling the battle hour-by-hour, and that's how I spent July 1, 2, 3, 1963: re-living the battle in my mind. We did go that year, but later in the season.

Fredericksburg was a natural side trip from Gettysburg. Even as a teenager, I was astounded at the casualties. The handbook for the area was entitled, *Where 100,000 Fell*, meaning the fighting in and around Fredericksburg cost 19th Century America 100,000 of its sons, killed, wounded, or missing.

I discovered there were four major battles fought within ten or twelve miles of Fredericksburg, and that the city became a vast hospital for many of those casualties. The backyards of the populace became temporary gravesites for those who died. I also learned that the history of Fredericksburg is broad and deep, which may account for the relative distillation and de-emphasis on the Civil War heritage of the town.

In spite of Gettysburg historians' attempts to assure everyone that there was a history of Gettysburg on June 30, 1863, and for a good sixty or so years before that date, no one, seemingly, wants to hear about it. July 1, 2, 3, 1863 (and maybe a little about the aftermath of the battle), is all virtually anyone who visits Gettysburg will hear about.

Fredericksburg has a rich tapestry of history, nearly as old as the first permanent English settlement in Jamestown, as vibrant in Colonial culture and economics as anything in Williamsburg, and as steeped in the Revolution as Philadelphia by being the boyhood home of George Washington.

How is Fredericksburg different from Gettysburg? Quite simply, the area has more history, more battles, and, as I found, more haunted sites.

GENERAL HISTORICAL BACKGROUND

Fredericksburg Skyline

Fredericksburg's recorded history dates back to 1608, when John Smith explored the Rappahannock River as far as the falls. Of course, Native Americans populated the area for centuries before, using the falls for fishing. Because the falls restricted large cargo ships from going any farther upstream, the town of Fredericksburg was created in 1728 as a port on the river.

Fredericksburg was named after the son of the English King George II and the streets still bear the names of Frederick's family members. Thus you have quaint, antiquated names for the streets such as Sophia (pronounced with a long "i" rather than the "e" sound), Caroline, Princess Anne, and Prince Edward Streets.

From the ages of six to sixteen George Washington lived just across the river at "Ferry Farm." In 1774 he sold Ferry Farm and moved his mother to a house which still stands on Charles Street in the city of Fredericksburg. His only sister, Betty, married Fielding Lewis, owner of what was to become Kenmore and who lost considerable personal fortune manufacturing arms for the American rebels (commanded by his brother-in-law) during the Revolution. Washington was friends with William Fitzhugh, who built "Chatham" the mansion that overlooks Fredericksburg from Stafford Heights. "I have put my legs oftener under your mahogany at Chatham than anywhere else in the world," Washington wrote to Fitzhugh. Throughout much of the rest of his life, Washington continued to visit his mother, friends, and other relatives in Fredericksburg.

After the Revolution, Fredericksburg continued to grow.

By 1835, Fredericksburg was home to about 3,000 residents, including whites, slaves, and free blacks. A canal, a turnpike and "plank" road, and a railroad were built to connect the town with the west. Within two years a railroad came in from Richmond, and the Rappahannock River continued to provide transportation between Fredericksburg and Baltimore. But by 1860, things in Fredericksburg were about to change radically because of its location.

FREDERICKSBURG AND THE CIVIL WAR

When Richmond became the capital of the Confederacy, Fredericksburg found itself on the direct route from Washington, seat of the Federal army, and its objective, Richmond. In November and December of 1862, the Union Army of the Potomac, under Major General Ambrose Burnside, situated on the east side of the Rappahannock, prepared to cross the river on pontoon bridges. The Confederate Army of Northern Virginia, commanded by General Robert E. Lee, dug in on the heights behind Fredericksburg. In the foggy early morning hours of December 11, 1862, Confederate soldiers from Mississippi, stationed at the river, began hearing suspicious sounds. At dawn the Union bridge-builders were discovered and Confederate marksmen drove them from their work leaving dead and dying Yankees on the unfinished bridge and floating down the Rappahannock.

Union artillery from across the river bombarded the town in an attempt to drive out the Mississippians. For eight hours General Burnside dropped shells into Fredericksburg, destroying many buildings, knocking holes in walls and setting fire to civilian homes. Even some churches were holed by Union shot. Still, the Mississippians clung tenaciously to their shelters along the riverside. Finally, at 3:00 P.M., Union soldiers rowed across the river in pontoons and drove the rebels from their positions in a 19th Century version of an "amphibious assault."

Still the Confederates refused to give up the town and house-to-house fighting ensued. The fighting was the most intense along Hawke, Caroline, and Princess Anne Streets. For almost two hours Confederates held their positions in the buildings, cellars and barricades between houses. With the Confederates thus occupied, the Northerners completed their bridges. The Union line eventually extended from Pitt Street to William Street. When the bridges near the City Dock were completed, the Southerners were flanked and under the cover of darkness, retreated to Marye's Heights.

FREDERICKSBURG AND THE PARANORMAL

Fredericksburg became the centerpiece for four of the major battles of the American Civil War: Fredericksburg in December 1862; Chancellorsville in May 1863; the Wilderness and Spotsylvania in the spring of 1864. What does the battle history of the town have to do with ghosts? Most of the buildings were scenes of deadly conflict, and the very streets were fought through. Both armies left dead and wounded strewn along the very paths you walk in Fredericksburg. Of the hundreds of buildings here during Civil War years, some 350 remain, many perhaps holding forever the spirits of the slain.

As well, 400 years of human history has resulted in countless restless, perturbed spirits. According to John Hennessy, the National Park Service Chief Historian at Fredericksburg, research into newspaper death records shows that over 100,000 people have died in and around Fredericksburg since the town's inception; yet, today there are only some 5,000 graves in the same area. Where are these people? Can they possibly rest in peace?

*   *   *

Since 1964, I've collected some 1,000 ghost stories from the battlefield of Gettysburg, the town of Gettysburg, and its environs. Like any sociological study, that much data begged extrapolation. A look at the types of paranormal experiences reveals the fact that, in Gettysburg, only about 10–11 percent of all the ghostly happenings are visual in nature. That is why so many people believe they've never had a paranormal experience. Asked, "Have *you* ever seen a ghost?" most people, compelled by honesty, will answer, "No." That doesn't mean, however, that they haven't had a paranormal experience. *All* the senses are involved. Based on my research, most paranormal events at Gettysburg are auditory (about 60–61 percent), with the remaining spread out between olfactory, tactile, and "feelings."

Fredericksburg, Virginia, and its environs, reveals two things. First is that so many of the sightings occurred to Civil War era individuals who witnessed ghosts from an earlier era, as opposed to Gettysburg ghost stories, which are almost entirely of modern individuals experiencing ghosts from the Civil War era. The second is that a cursory examination of the hundred or so stories of Fredericksburg of which I am aware, leads me to calculate that about 25 percent of all the stories *are visual in nature,* twice as many visuals as in Gettysburg.

The point being: if you want to hear a ghost, go to Gettysburg; if you want to *see* a ghost, come to Fredericksburg.

What could be the reason?

Paranormal investigators have, for decades, realized that those in the spirit world need energy in order to manifest themselves. Fresh batteries in cameras die moments after being taken into an allegedly haunted area; even expensive television camera batteries—three "belts" of batteries, one after the other—died when they were set on the ground in the infamous Triangular Field at Gettysburg. Lights flicker in the presence of paranormal energy. Paranormal investigators and mediums find themselves exhausted after an investigation: the spirits will steal energy from anywhere, including, apparently, from the researchers.

Marsh Creek is the largest body of flowing water that runs through the Gettysburg area. Sachs Covered Bridge, which spans Marsh Creek near the south end of the battlefield is well known for its high amount of paranormal activity. Perhaps it is not just coincidence.

Rappahannock River

The Rappahannock River runs parallel to Fredericksburg. And, while the river appears to be slow moving, it generates an incredible amount of energy, from its sheer mass, as it lumbers its way toward the Chesapeake Bay. The Rappahannock River carries ten times the amount of water as Marsh Creek. Most of Fredericksburg lies within a dozen blocks of the river. If there ever was a never-ending supply from which to draw energy, it is certainly the Rappahannock. Apparently, it takes the most energy for a disembodied spirit to manifest itself as a full-body apparition (as opposed to an "orb," or a noise, the most common manifestations). It is my opinion that the energy from the Rappahannock accounts for why Fredericksburg has so many visual paranormal events. That latent energy, as well as the longer history, may be the two main reasons that, *per capita*, Fredericksburg has more ghost stories involving apparitions than Gettysburg.

A BRIEF INTRODUCTION TO THE PARANORMAL

What is a Ghost?

According to Rosemary Ellen Guiley in her *Encyclopedia of Ghosts and Spirits*, quite simply, a ghost is an alleged spirit of the dead. The age-old definition is that a ghost is a disembodied soul, which, after the life of its body is over, goes on to live an existence apart from the visible world. Renowned ghost hunter Hans Holzer's definition adds a more sinister twist: "ghosts are the surviving mental faculties of people who died traumatically." This would apply to just about every soldier who died at Fredericksburg.

How Spirits Manifest

First, it is important to remember that all the human senses are involved in perceiving ghosts. Many people must admit that they have never seen a ghost. People report seeing translucent orbs, ropey mists, and full-body apparitions—sometimes light and sometimes dark—that look like live humans. Often these images are seen "out of the corner of the eye," in one's peripheral vision. A good 60–61 percent of all paranormal experiences are auditory—including footsteps where it is known no human walks—moans, murmurings, shouts, and screams. (At Spotsylvania's Bloody Angle, while attempting to record EVP, I heard distinctly from the woodline across the field, a brief crackling sound that could only be likened to the "rattle" of musketry. Unfortunately, the recorder did not pick it up.) But, other senses are involved, including the sense of smell. People have reported smelling tobacco smoke while alone in an open field, or wood smoke when there is no campfire nearby. Rosewater and lilac (Victorian era perfumes) that were used to cover up the stench of decaying bodies can sometimes be smelled, as well. Other people report being touched or tapped on the shoulder by an invisible entity. And finally, many people just get a certain "feeling" that they are not alone, or that they are being stared at when in an allegedly haunted place.

Virtually all major religions preach some sort of afterlife and some proof of human's belief in an afterlife may pre-date organized religion. Some 70,000 years ago, proto-humans buried their dead with implements, tools, clothes, weapons, food and water for a journey. Did one—or several—of the dead re-visit them as ghosts to make it seem logical to supply them for a journey?

CLASSIFICATIONS OF GHOSTS

Intelligent Hauntings

An intelligent haunting is one in which the entity seems to have a consciousness and will interact with the living.

The Woman in White of St. George's Episcopal Church—Fredericksburg.

St. George's Episcopal Church is located on Princess Anne Street. St. George's Episcopal congregation is the oldest continuing congregation in Fredericksburg and once included George Washington. The current church building was erected in 1849 and supplanted the earlier structure on the same site. This event happened in 1858. Miss Ella McCarty was accompanying a young man to choir practice. Miss McCarty and her friend were early for practice and the church was cold and dark. The only other occupant was the organist. The organist and Miss McCarty's friend went to find more than the two candles they carried, while she ascended to the choir loft. As her eyes grew accustomed to the low light, she realized that, apparently, someone else was in the church with her. She saw a woman dressed all in white kneeling at the alter praying. But something just didn't seem right about the kneeling woman. Within a few seconds, the woman arose, turned to head back down the aisle, and suddenly looked up at Miss McCarty. Upon seeing her, the woman in white vanished into thin air, as if reacting to being discovered.

The Devil's Den Ghost—Gettysburg. A young woman had gotten lost in Devil's Den early one morning. She parked her car and resigned herself to taking some pictures before finding her way out. With the camera to her eye, she suddenly got a "feeling" that she was not alone. Turning around, she saw a man she described as disheveled—long, tangled hair, large, floppy hat, ragged shirt and pants, and barefoot. He looked at her and pointed back over her shoulder. "What you're looking for," he said in a distinctly southern accent, "is over there." She turned impulsively to see what he was pointing at, suddenly realized that he couldn't know what she was looking for, and turned back to confront... nothing. The figure, after interacting with her, completely vanished!

Imprints, or Residual Hauntings

An Imprint or Residual Haunting is when a spirit appears to mindlessly repeat its actions periodically through the years, oblivious to its surroundings or any living beings who attempt to communicate with it.

The Ghost in Kenmore—Fredericksburg. There have been many sightings at Kenmore Mansion of the famed brother-in-law of George Washington, Fielding Lewis. Lewis was a prominent and prosperous citizen of Fredericksburg in the pre-Revolution era. He built one of the finer homes in the city, now called "Kenmore." At the request of the fledgling American congress, he produced thousands of muskets for the army. When they couldn't pay him, he continued to manufacture the weapons, relying upon the promise of payment once independence was won. But even after the war was over, the payment never came. Fielding Lewis lost a fortune and spent the rest of his life (and apparently some time after) worrying about paying for his magnificent home. To this day there are reports of the sighting of a man dressed in 18th Century garb in one of the side rooms of the mansion, with a worried expression upon his face, poring over financial ledgers, oblivious to the observer.

The Suicidal Ghost—Fredericksburg. Smythe's Cottage, on Fauquier Street, just off Princess Anne, was the scene of at least two types of hauntings, one of which appears to be an imprint. The story circulated that the woman who lived in the house with her husband during the Civil War became a Union sympathizer, perhaps because her husband had joined the Confederate Army and was away much of the time from a city occupied by Yankees. Of course, more sinister rumors about the woman, whom some have named "Elizabeth," have circulated about her "entertaining" the Yankees in her home. After the war, when her husband returned, he heard the rumors and confronted her. Overcome by shame, she apparently hanged herself at the top of the stairs. In recent years, Smythe's Cottage has housed a restaurant. In addition to other unexplainable phenomena, such as lighted candles being blown out and silverware moved about by someone unseen, there is the report that, during a paranormal investigation, a patron watched as a woman dressed in Civil War attire, ran past him without so much as a glance, and disappeared into the garden. Investigators immediately followed, but found no trace of her, even though the garden was surrounded by a high fence.

Courtesy of Kathleen Butcher

Smythe's Cottage

The Pry House Ghost—Antietam. Fought on September 17, 1862, Antietam (named by the Federals after a local creek) or Sharpsburg (named after the nearby town in Maryland by the Confederates) was the bloodiest single day in American History, costing both sides some 23,000 casualties.

Another casualty not listed in the military records was Mrs. Pry, whose husband owned a house on the battlefield. The war ruined them financially, and some say, ruined Mrs. Pry mentally. Long after she had died and her home had come into the ownership of the National Park Service, the interior of the house was gutted by fire. During the reconstruction, when only the stairway to the second floor was completed, three or four workmen and the foreman's wife were standing in the hall. They saw an elderly woman descend the stairs and walk between them to the exterior or the house. They noticed two things about her: she had long blonde hair, and she was translucent. She was oblivious to the workmen, the foreman's wife, and her surroundings, doing what she had done hundreds of times when she owned the house; a perfect example of an imprint, or residual haunting.

There may have been another sighting of Mrs. Pry. Two Park Rangers were on patrol one night shortly after the Pry House had burned. They stopped in front of the darkened house tragically gutted by fire a few months before. No doubt they were upset at the loss of the entire interior, but were thankful that the brick exterior walls had survived. They were stunned and a bit perplexed to see a wraith-like figure of what was obviously a woman in a long, flowing gown center itself in a second-floor window. They saw her, but they obviously saw the impossible. With the floor missing, to be looking out of that window, she would have to be standing on thin air.

Rips in Time, or Warps

One of the most mysterious of all paranormal phenomena is the warp, an apparent rip in the fabric of time, which allows one to see into a scene from the past. By definition, almost any ghostly encounter, as long as it involves the spirit of a person from the past, can be classified as a warp. Scenes of soldiers from a bygone era, marching through a field where soldiers once marched in battle can be considered warps. When warps occur inside a man-made portal, such as a doorway or window, the scene is amplified.

St. George's Episcopal Church—Fredericksburg. Courage is often defined not as the absence of fear, but of knowing the danger, yet overcoming one's fear to perform one's duty. Such would certainly seem the case with the Fredericksburg Police and St. George's Episcopal Church.

St. George's Episcopal Church around Fredericksburg.

The church has been a landmark since 1849. The steeple appears in Civil War era photographs and is referenced in numerous contemporary accounts of the battle and its aftermath. It was used as a temporary hospital, as were most of the churches in the city. But unlike the other churches, the pews are fastened to the floor within heat-holding half-walls and so were not torn out and used as headboards for the dead. There are accounts, however, of the fence outside the church draped with cartridge boxes, belts, knapsacks, and canteens of the wounded sufferers within, and of the dead piled up like cordwood on either side of the front steps into the church as high as the top step. Horror and human trauma were no strangers to St. George's during the battles

In many ways, Fredericksburg maintains the genteel habits and customs of an America of an earlier time. The doors to the churches—at least at St. George's—stay open to anyone who wishes to worship privately until 9:00 P.M., then are locked for the night. The police still check doors after hours to make sure all is well. Occasionally, the doors to the church will be found unlocked after 9:00 P.M. Whether someone just forgot to lock them in the first place, or they were somehow unlocked, is never discovered. The police readily admit, almost to a man, that, when they've checked the church after hours, strange things have happened.

Periodically, an officer will be checking the sanctuary and hear footsteps coming up the aisle. Turning to confront whoever comes to worship after hours reveals no one visible. The wooden half-walls around the pews have short doors that open to allow worshippers in, then shut out the drafts. Officers have reported hearing one of the doors open—or shut—while they inspect the facility. (An invisible worshipper, no doubt!) The K-9 patrols especially dislike the interior of the church. Animals, for a number of reasons, seem to be more sensitive to the supernatural. The dogs especially avoid the stairs to the choir loft. And finally, there is the story of the rookie policeman who was paired with a veteran for the evening patrol. They stopped in front of St. George's Church. The rookie told the veteran he would check the door. Sure enough, the door was unlocked, and the young policeman signaled that he would check it out.

Five minutes passed. Then ten. Just as the veteran was about to go in to see what had happened to the young officer, he emerged from the church, rattled the door to make sure it was locked, and returned to the patrol car.

"Is everything okay?" asked the veteran.

"I checked the place from top to bottom," was the reply. "I even checked that weird red room. That place is really strange."

The problem lies in the fact that there is no red room in St. George's Church. But there is, evidently, a good example of a paranormal warp.

Smythe's Cottage, Revisited—Fredericksburg. And finally, we return to Smythe's Cottage, home of "Elizabeth," who hanged herself at the top of the stairs. There have been a number of people, guests, customers, and employees, who have passed the open doorway to the second floor and noticed the most bizarre vision through that portal: first out of the corner of their eye they see it slowly moving, side to side; then they reluctantly glance up. There, at the top of the stairs is the full apparition of a woman, neck bent at an unnatural angle, swaying, feet dangling just above the stairs. Then she de-materializes.

Poltergeist Activity

"Poltergeist" is the German word for "noisy ghost," a paranormal energy that moves or throws objects, slams doors, flicks lights on and off, and generally causes mischief. Since poltergeist activity has often been recorded in the presence of young adolescents, particularly women, some researchers attribute it to the energy of the living being so strong that it actually moves objects. A great deal of poltergeist activity occurs in college atmospheres as well, since young men and women, aged 18 to 21, have been know to have high energy levels. If this is true, the paranormal activity cannot justifiably be attributed to a "ghost," but to some energy outreach force of the living. But it is not entirely proven that adolescent women are the source.

The Kenmore Inn—Fredericksburg. There is a stately antebellum mansion on Princess Anne Street, the Kenmore Inn, which is currently a Bed and Breakfast. The land was originally owned by the family of Fielding Lewis back in the 1740s. The building likely dates back to before the War of 1812. During the Battle of Fredericksburg in December of 1862, the house was heavily shelled. The cellar, now a modern restaurant and bar, was used by Federals for stabling their horses and some of the out-buildings were used as quarters for the Federal wounded.

Several instances of poltergeist activity have been recorded within the walls of the mansion. A woman staying in room 208 was awakened at 3:00 A.M. by the sound of something of great weight and bulk being dragged down the hall. She likened it not to modern wheeled luggage, but to something of great mass being wrestled along the hallway. (My first thought, from her description, was that it was the sound of a human body being dragged through the hall. But, I'm willing to admit, perhaps the history of the place as a hospital got to me.) She distinctly heard it pass her door, but then the noise stopped before it reached the stairs. Checking with the management the next morning revealed that no one had left in the middle of the night. Later, the same woman was staying in room 107. She was in the bathroom and went out to the bed to get something from her suitcase. When she returned to the bathroom a few seconds later, the light had been switched off. Now employed at the inn, she gets reports from guests staying in room 107 that the medicine cabinet door very often pops open by itself and the bathroom door will not stay closed. The door will be latched and, as if someone unseen feels trapped in the bathroom, spontaneously bursts open.

There's a back room at the inn which she has stayed in that seems to be active with "poltergeists." A sound is heard like the banging of pipes when the heat is turned on, a "metal on metal" sound as she describes it. She heard the metallic sounds emanating from the floor of that room, night after night, clanking, like someone beating on the pipes. There is only one problem: the room is unheated, and there are no pipes below the floor to make any sound.

In room 207, something continues to knock a picture off the wall in the bathroom. Returned to its place securely on the nail behind the commode, the picture will later end up sitting behind the commode on the floor. The nail, however, remains solidly imbedded in the hard plaster wall. As well, the picture, which has a glass covering and light wooden frame, is never broken. It is almost as if someone just doesn't like the picture in that room, and casually removes it and sets it, undamaged, upon the floor.

Smythe's Cottage Once Again—Fredericksburg. For more poltergeist activity, we must return to Smythe's Cottage, where "Elizabeth," apparently driven to self destruction by shame, hanged herself in the upstairs hallway. Witnesses have confirmed the destruction of a sugar container, placed upon one of the tables. Suddenly, and for no earthly reason, it was flung to the floor and shattered by an invisible hand. In addition, there is the portrait of General Ulysses S. Grant which hangs in the back serving room. One morning, the owners opened the building and found the portrait hanging upside down on the wall. They returned it to its natural position, but subsequently have found it hanging crookedly. They straighten it, only to find it askew later on. Finally, they gave up, and the picture hangs crookedly, a concession perhaps, to a Confederate veteran who once owned the house, betrayed in the cruelest way possible, by the woman he loved.

Crises Apparitions

A Crises Apparition is when a spirit returns to impart important information to the living. Often, the apparition is of a close acquaintance or loved one.

The Aquia Church Harbinger—Fredericksburg. One of the more haunted sites in the area is Aquia Church. The original Aquia Church was built in 1751, and, curiously, burned in 1751. The second and current church was built in 1757 by William Copein, a mason, and Mourning Richards, an appropriately named undertaker. Sometime during the tumultuous years of the American Revolution, "murder most foul" was committed in the place where the living go for spiritual refreshment, on the very floor under which early parishioners lie buried awaiting the promised resurrection. For almost two hundred years, until it was covered over by reinforcing cement, one of the flagstones in the floor of the center aisle of Aquia Church was stained by the blood of a young woman, killed in the sanctuary. The murdered woman's body was hidden in the belfry. The church had been abandoned for a number of years after that, so the body went undetected until, when it was finally discovered, there was nothing left but a hoary skeleton with long blonde hair still attached to a grinning skull.

Always, always, if you want to confirm a ghost story, consult the locals, for it is they who have to live with the consequences of the unsettled dead. And so, it has been rumored that not even the bravest of Stafford County have been able to force themselves to approach Aquia Church near midnight, for it is then that the sounds begin.

The noises are so loud, so distinct, that they can even be heard by those brave enough to merely walk past the church at night. Reports claim that, from within the ancient walls can be heard "heavy noises" indicative of a struggle inside; as well, there are discerned the sounds of feet running up, then down the stairs to the belfry. If the passerby is brave enough to enter the church, all sounds immediately cease.

Sometime prior to the 1930s, a woman who was interested in the supernatural determined that she would document any evidence that Aquia Church was haunted. Since midnight was the hour at which paranormal activities allegedly began, that is when she would conduct her investigation. But, try as she might, she could get no one in Stafford County to accompany her. She finally recruited two investigators from Washington, D. C., so that they might witness and record any anomalies that were reputed to happen within the church. They arrived just before midnight, and the woman was soon to discover that there were more than mere auditory apparitions present in Aquia Church, for no sooner had she set foot in the church when a hand slapped her hard in the face. Hearing the hard blow and her scream, the other investigators rushed past her, but could find no one else in the church. With the addition of violence, the investigation suddenly ended. They left, but for days afterward, the red mark of the phantom hand remained upon her face. A visitor to Aquia from Washington, while inspecting the church one evening, realized that the door was unlocked. He inquired of a local resident and complimented the person on what a trusting community they must have, never to have to lock the doors of their church. The reason the doors to the church were unlocked, the man explained, is because, no matter how many times they are locked, they simply will not stay locked. It is as if someone needs continual access in and out of the church.

Earlier in the 20th Century there were persistent reports of the sighting of a young woman, with long blonde hair, periodically peering out the windows of the church. Fed up with what he thought were silly superstitions, one of the men of the neighborhood decided he would prove to the others that there was nothing to be frightened of, and that they were all just being babies. He said he would climb to the belfry that night. They teased him and said that he would probably just go into the doorway, wait a minute or two, then emerge, merely claiming he had visited the dreaded belfry. He would show them. He took a hammer and a nail out of his truck and into the church; he would climb to the belfry and hammer the nail into the wood there as evidence he had visited; they could check his work the next morning ... or whenever they gathered enough courage.

He entered the church and his friends waited outside, laughing nervously. Ten minutes passed. Then twenty. They began to call softly to him. Was he all right? Come on now, he could come out. The joke was over.

Forty minutes pass, and his friends are beginning to worry. Did he fall and hurt himself? Is he inside that awful place, unconscious, bleeding perhaps? His friends summoned their courage. By the time they got some lanterns, a good hour had passed and still, nothing from their friend. They went inside, half wondering at every corner, if their friend was about to jump out and give them the fright of their lives. They were shocked when they finally reached the belfry. There was their friend, hammer lying next to him, his eyes frozen open, his mouth contorted into a silenced scream. In the dark he had hammered the nail through his own coat and into the wood of the belfry. When he tried to leave, it must have felt as if something had grabbed him and held him fast. Believing it was whatever evil that resides within the church that had imprisoned him and refused to let him go, his heart gave out and he died of fright. Aquia Church had claimed another victim.

But the crises apparition occurred during the Civil War. William Fitzhugh from Fredericksburg was a Confederate soldier. He and a fellow soldier had been scouting the area of Aquia. They were exhausted and decided to spend the night, in spite of its reputation of being haunted, in the antiquated church. They decided they would leave the door open so they might hear any activity outside. Curled up in the pews, they began what would be a restless night. Sometime after midnight, they were both awakened by the shuffling of feet on the flagstones at the rear of the church. Both were immediately awake, but hidden by the pews. Could it be a Yankee? Then, the whistling began. Eventually, they recognized the ancient tune: "The Campbells are Coming." Then it stopped. Then the steps were even closer, halfway up the aisle, and the whistling started again. The two young men looked at each other in the dark, afraid to peek over the pew. The whistling stopped. Again, this time, right next to them, came the footsteps. And finally, again, the whistling. Together they leapt from the pew and struck a match to find … nothing before them. But, from the road in front of the church they heard the unmistakable sound of Yankee cavalrymen. Fully awake, thanks to the frightening footsteps and ghostly whistling, they crawled out the back windows of the church, found their horses, and rode off, convinced they had been saved by the timely appearance of a ghost.

Ghost Lights

For centuries, strange lights have been seen from a distance on the ocean, in fields and marshes, upon mountainsides, and in the air. When approached, they simply disappear.

Fairy Lights—In folklore. Before there was such a thing as "light pollution," strange tales of unexplainable lights across the moors and fields of rural areas were reported. Attributing the lights to fairies flitting about, they were so named: Fairy Lights. Were they methane gas? The descriptions indicate that they were much more animated than "swamp gas" which will glow, but certainly not flit around as if alive. If anything, their description is more like, what paranormal investigators have named, "orbs."

Orbs—In every ghost hunter's camera. "Orbs" are believed to be some remnant of spirit energy and are probably the most commonly misidentified type of paranormal phenomena captured on film. An orb on film looks like a white (or occasionally colored), semi-translucent circle of light, often with a sort of "nucleus" in the center. They can be captured by just about any kind of camera, from cheap 35 mm throw-aways to high-end digitals. They are often photographed in areas known for their history and paranormal activity. There seems to be a high percentage of orbs in photos of family members during celebrations, such as weddings, children's birthdays, and holiday gatherings, leading one to conclude that the orb in question is the spirit of a deceased family member "attending" the festivities.

We cannot be entirely certain that orbs are ghosts—the spirit energy of dead individuals. What we do know is that they exhibit several characteristics that lead us to believe that they are actually energy. First, they can be detected by quick-read thermometers, usually with a drop in temperature, but sometimes with a rise in temperature as well. My wife, Carol, took a photo of me detecting a cold spot while testing a quick-read thermometer in the Ghosts of Gettysburg Tour building. I moved the probe to the right and the indicator dropped; I moved the probe back and the temperature rose. The third time this happened, I asked Carol to take a picture. There, next to the probe in the picture, is a small orb which I was evidently picking up with the quick-read thermometer.

Orbs also appear to have electromagnetic qualities to them. People have taken photographs of them after an EMF (electromagnetic field meter) has activated. Also, they seem to move with some intelligence, often responding to requests or commands. Such purposeful actions by any entity that sometimes defy the laws of classical physics cannot be dismissed.

Some investigators attribute the "chill," or "gooseflesh," one gets at a haunted site to the electricity from orbs passing over the hairs on one's skin.

Orbs can be photographed with either "night-shot" exposure or regular flash. The question is, are they merely reflecting the light or are they self-illuminating in response to the flash or infrared, like bio-luminescent, living sea-creatures?

Then, again, orbs are the easiest to fake—or mistake. Dust, mist, rain, snow, hair, lint, and certain insects, if close enough to the lens of an automatic-focus camera (which is already focusing on something in the distance) can all appear as orbs. The larger the lens, the more likely a piece of dust has wandered in front of it. Some credit-card sized cameras have tiny, pinhole lenses and the possibility of a piece of dust floating before the tiny lens at just the time a photo is being snapped is much less likely. Sometimes the only way to be sure the orb you've captured on film is a spirit, is to eliminate all the other possibilities. This is why documenting the investigative session, either on paper or by recording it with a video camera, is so important. Keep all the details associated with the investigation—time, temperature, relative humidity, pollen count, weather conditions—so that bogus causes of orbs can be ruled out.

There are times when you can be pretty much assured that what you've captured is a true anomaly: orbs that appear partially behind something which is at a distance—such as a tree or fence-post—can obviously not be anything too close to the lens to be out-of-focus. A moving orb that is seen on video coming *through* a wall, is obviously not a dust particle.

Orbs seen with the naked eye are obviously not faked. My own experience is illustrative.

Rick Fisher, Director of the Pennsylvania Paranormal Society, had taken me out to Sachs Covered Bridge southwest of Gettysburg for an investigation. At this point, even though I had written two books on ghosts at Gettysburg, I was still an extreme skeptic, especially where orbs were involved. I was sure they were simply pieces of dust, casually drifting in front of the camera lens which was focused upon something in the distance. As we stood at the end of the bridge nearest the parking area, he handed me his night vision scope and said, "I want you to look down the length of the bridge."

I stood with my eye pressed to the eyepiece for at least a minute. Nothing happened. "What am I looking for?" I asked Rick. "You'll know when you see it," he said confidently.

Within a few more seconds I was again becoming bored. Suddenly, I saw it.

A huge ball of light came through—*through*—the roof of the bridge, paused briefly before my face, did a 90 degree turn to the left, and flashed at an incalculable speed out through the side of the bridge. As the saying goes, you could have knocked me over with a feather.

I no doubt issued an explicative at which Rick laughed, then smiled knowingly.

From that moment I knew that true "orbs" were something completely different from anything else I had ever encountered.

In another instance, a fellow investigator watched an orb come through the windshield of my van, float between us and move to the back of the van. She took a picture. There in the back of the van was the orb, suspended near the back door.

Why Spirits Linger

According to Psychic Pam Saylor, spirits once attached to a human will remain upon the earth (as opposed to "going toward the light"—the universal light of the afterlife) for the following reasons:

A sudden death.
An unexpected death.
A youthful death.
A violent extinction.
Leaving something unresolved in life.
To give a message of good or ill.
The living are mourning too long.
Fear of judgment.

Virtually every soldier who died during the battles around Fredericksburg experienced one or more of these types of death: sudden, unexpected, youthful, violent, leaving an unresolved life. As far as remaining to give a message, perhaps they are trying to give an age-old message about the futility of war and human strife. According to the National Park Service figures, about 1.2 million people come to the area every year to study the battle; in essence, to mourn those who fought and died here. With Christianity being the major religion in Victorian America, and its tenet against fratricide, it is easy to see why the soldiers who fought here were, and perhaps still are fearful of final judgment.

WHY DO GHOSTS EXIST?

There are a number of theories that attempt to explain why ghosts exist. The theories range from explaining ghosts as merely a figment of one's imagination or a hallucination, to intricate mathematical theories based upon the science of physics.[1]

The Unconsecrated Burial Theory

One traditional explanation for the existence of ghosts that certainly applies to Fredericksburg (and other Civil War battlefields) is the Unconsecrated Burial Theory.

Many religions encompass the belief that, if a person is buried without a ceremony consecrating the ground and with words to help the deceased move on to the Other World, the spirit is doomed to remain earthbound. At Fredericksburg (and Chancellorsville, The Wilderness, and Spotsylvania Court House) the dead from the battles received at least two burials. The first burial was on the battlefield, usually near where they died; the second burial came months—and sometimes years—later, after locals complained about the shallow, hastily dug graves opening to the rain and scavengers. Federal officials purchased land, exhumed the bodies, and, as in the case of Union soldiers, reburied them in one large cemetery, many of which became "National Cemeteries." I limit this explanation to Federal soldiers, because, as in the case of Gettysburg, Confederate soldiers were "the enemy." They were left buried on the battlefield, near where they fell, until the early 1870s, when social groups from the defunct Confederacy (usually women, since so many of the men never made it back from the war) made contact with someone at the battlefields in the north and solicited them to exhume the Confederate bodies and send them south. After some six or seven years, unembalmed, with nothing but a blanket for a coffin, the remains of Southern soldiers were sent, several to a box, back to the old Confederacy, for which they made the ultimate sacrifice. Finally, the dead from Gettysburg were buried in consecrated ground in some of the major cemeteries in the South such as Hollywood Cemetery in Richmond, Virginia, and Laurel Grove Cemetery in Savannah, Georgia.

When a battle was fought in the South, as so many were, the fallen Southerners had a better chance of being buried in consecrated ground sooner rather than later. And yet, with so many of the battlefields ending up within the scope of the Northern occupation, many remained in unconsecrated graves for quite a while.

During the first Battle of Fredericksburg in December 1862, the vast majority of the casualties were Union. Organized burial parties from both sides appear to have begun their work late in the day on December 15 at the Slaughter Pen, on the Bowling Green Road about two miles south of Fredericksburg.

The day had been balmy, but due to officers requiring a properly documented truce, burials did not begin until there was barely an hour of daylight left. Nevertheless, burial details from opposite sides met at the picket lines and began burying the dead in mass graves. Sunset put a premature end to the work and heaps of bodies remained where they had been gathered. Some Confederates shoved their comrades' mortal remains down into the railroad embankment and kicked the earth down the slope upon the corpses, a makeshift and unconsecrated sepulture indeed.[2]

Later that evening, the Union retreat across the Rappahannock began. By 3:00 A.M. on December 16, the last Northern combat troops had crossed, leaving behind their dead. Within an hour or so of the pontoons being taken up, some Confederates began re-occupying the city and later found that fresh graves scarred nearly every yard. In front of Marye's Heights, a Confederate officer reported that, although he had been on hotly contested battlefields before where he thought the dead lay in heaps, there appeared more dead to the acre than anywhere else he had seen. One Southerner totaled 484 bodies in one acre; another observed that a man could walk within 600 square yards and not be able to find ground upon which to place his foot. One Confederate staff officer estimated 800 bodies just in front of Marye's Heights, and yet another thought the field appeared covered in blue cloth. Closer, more sickening inspection revealed that men were disemboweled, dismembered, decapitated, and mutilated so badly that they were virtually beyond recognition as human beings. At dawn on December 17, by a pre-arranged truce, Union Army burial parties crossed the river back into Fredericksburg and began their onerous task.

Long trenches—some necessarily shallow because the ground was frozen—were dug and bodies gathered. Many had been stripped of their clothing by needy Confederates. Some of the dead had frozen hard to the ground; pick axes had to be used to free them. The shallow trenches and frozen earth made the mass burials overly crowded. Even Confederate commander Robert E. Lee expressed his annoyance to Union chief Burnside at the treatment of his enemy's dead, but nothing was done. Some of the Union soldiers detailed to bury the dead, as some soldiers will, found the easy way out and threw scores of bodies into a nearby ice house, to be found years later.

Colonel John R. Brooke, in charge of the burials, counted 620 bodies interred near Marye's Heights before his group made their way back across the river for the night. The next day they returned to bury another 400. As horrific as the butchery was on this sector of the field, a Virginia soldier thought the fighting before Prospect Hill, while less concentrated, was more terrible in the slaughter of humans.[3]

In 1866, the War Department in Washington, faced with the fact that Fredericksburg had been the epicenter of four major battles between December 1862 and May 1864—just 18 months—and the 15,000 dead Union soldiers those battles cast off, decided to gather the men buried in solitary graves and mass pits, and consolidate them into a large "national" cemetery on Marye's Heights. For two years the farm wagons *cum* hearses rolled in from the fields in front of Marye's Heights and Prospect Hill, from the tangled, charred underbrush of the Wilderness, from the trenches near Spotsylvania Court House. The earth was opened and what was left of the Union soldiers was buried upon the terraced slope of the hill they sought in battle, but never gained except in death.

But what had happened to the Confederate soldiers? How long did they wait for burial in consecrated soil?

The Ladies Memorial Association of Fredericksburg was formed on May 10, 1865, with the purpose to procure funds to purchase land for a cemetery for the Southern soldiers who had been killed in the battles in the vicinity of the city and in Spotsylvania County. By 1867 they had purchased land next to the Fredericksburg Cemetery where Amelia Street dead-ends into Washington Avenue. The remains of more than 2,000 Confederate soldiers—most unknown—were brought to the burying ground and laid to rest. Among them are the bodies of six generals, and one female soldier, Lucy Ann Cox, buried with her husband whom she had accompanied in the 30th Virginia Infantry throughout four years of war, an "honorary" Confederate veteran. These Confederate dead—the ones they found and removed from their battlefield graves—finally lay in consecrated ground.

The Environmental Phenomena Theory

Another theory as to why ghosts exist is the Environmental Phenomena Theory. It is well-known among those who study the paranormal that the natural environment, as well as a sordid history, will contribute to the paranormal activity in an area. Often, where there is a great deal of quartz-bearing granite, there are more than the average number of ghost tales. Fredericksburg, like Gettysburg, is one such place. The theory is that the quartz in the rock, like the quartz crystal in your watch, vibrated to the electrical energy given off by soldiers in extreme emotional duress, wounded, dying, or fearful that they were about to be injured, like the soldier defending or attacking the stone wall in the Sunken Road.

Humans, as well as most other animals, are electrical creatures: our brains, when thinking hard, give off enough electricity to light a small bulb; our bodies respond to electrical stimuli to heal themselves; our bones, when broken violently, such as by a minie ball moving at 900 feet per second, give off piezo-electrical energy.

Charles J. Adams, III, author of dozens of regional ghost books, did an experiment. He took all of the ghost stories he had collected in Pennsylvania and charted them on a transparent mylar sheet placed over a map of the state. Then he found a map of iron deposits in Pennsylvania. He placed the mylar map over the map of iron deposits and discovered that they matched: it seems that where there was an abundance of iron, there was also an abundance of ghost stories. Was the electromagnetic energy given off by the dead and dying captured, like a magnetic image or recording, in the iron deposits?

This electromagnetic energy seems to be the basis for a number of postulations on manifestations of life after death—ghosts, in layman's terms. Some theorize the energy, however minute, is stored in the rocks, minerals—like iron—and wood in an historic area, particularly one where there was a lot of dying. Later, under certain conditions, it is released and sensed by living humans using any one or more of their senses. (The "certain conditions" can be anything from solar flares to passing thunderstorms to the energy brought to the area by the living human, as in poltergeist phenomena.) Some believe that the energy moves in little "packets," which show up in photos (or can be visualized by certain sensitives) as "orbs." The electromagnetic energy released from the environment, may be enough to produce auditory, olfactory, tactile, or even visual responses as it passes through (as electromagnetic energy does) the living human brain. This electromagnetic energy seems to be the reason why the alleged voices of the dead can be picked up on magnetic tape, or by digital recorders. This phenomena is called Electromagnetic Voice Phenomena, or "EVP," and is one of the more interesting aspects of investigating the paranormal. The gathering of EVP will be explained in another chapter.

As well, most paranormalists recognize that spirit entities need to "borrow" some amount of energy to manifest. Often they will borrow it from the batteries in cameras brought on the investigation site; sometimes the investigator themselves will be the source of stolen energy. We are still studying whether large energy surges created during solar flare-ups have an effect upon spirit manifestations. (Which is one more reason to record data—at least the date—during the investigation.) Ghost "touches," paranormal "smells," and unexplained noises and voices are manifestations that evidently take little energy since they are fairly common occurrences. Visual apparitions, on the other hand, seem to require large amounts of borrowed energy—they are the most infrequent manifestations.

Water—especially moving water—is an incredible source of energy. A cubic yard of water weighs 1685 pounds—1730 pounds if it is salt water. One can only imagine the vast amounts of energy available in a moving stream. The Rappahannock River, which runs past Fredericksburg is ten times the size of Marsh Creek in Gettysburg. Is it any wonder then, that Fredericksburg boasts more visual hauntings than Gettysburg?

HOW TO INVESTIGATE THE PARANORMAL

Since the publication of the book series *Ghosts of Gettysburg* there has been a rash of amateur "Ghost Investigators" swarming the fields of the National Park at Gettysburg, rushing from one place to another before the park closes. Some have even tried to sneak onto the National Park after closing, believing that the *only* haunted area in Gettysburg is enclosed by the National Park Service boundaries. Invariably, they've gotten caught, ticketed, and have managed to upset more than a few park rangers.

Worse, they've gotten photos of swarms of "orbs" in a field of floating pollen, or gasp at the "ectoplasm" they captured on film after quickly throwing away their cigarette, or marvel at the amazing "flesh-colored ghost" they swear is not their finger in front of the lens. All they've done is set back legitimate paranormal research for the mistaken ability to show their friends at home their own "Ghost of Gettysburg."

Investigating the paranormal at Fredericksburg is a little different.

First, there are more battlefields to investigate. Within twenty minutes' drive, four major battlefields of the American Civil War are available for investigation.

Second, by almost all accounts, the fighting in and around the Fredericksburg/Spotsylvania area of Virginia was even *more* violent, savage, and longer in duration than anything at Gettysburg—or anywhere else, for that matter.

In freezing December 1862, the Union soldiers must have conceived utter horror as they tried to cross the open Rappahannock River on narrow pontoon bridges with Confederates cutting them down from the shelter of the riverfront houses; at Chancellorsville, in the spring of 1863, Northerners felt complete panic as "Stonewall" Jackson's men broke from the woods and routed them like sheep until their backs were at the river; a year later, fighting through the tangled maze of the Wilderness filled the minds of the men with claustrophobic fear as they watched helplessly the wounded scream and cremate alive when the woods caught fire; and the men of both sides must have thought death a welcome respite just a few days later as they fought in the rain not more than a few yards apart for twenty-two hours straight at the Bloody Angle at Spotsylvania. Casualties for the Wilderness and Spotsylvania—in essence, one prolonged battle at two different venues—topped 60,000, the bloodiest battle in American History.

Suffice it to say, everything indicates that within a fifteen mile radius of the City of Fredericksburg, in Spotsylvania County, there exists more potential for hauntings than almost any other like-sized area in the entire United States.

Third, while some National Park-owned areas are closed after dusk, many other areas remain "drive through"—you may travel the roads after dark, but you may not park your car and get out. A photo only takes a second to record; video can be taken while you drive along; Electronic Voice Phenomena (EVP) is a little more difficult to get in a moving car, but not impossible.

But, many of the sites of violence—especially in Fredericksburg—occurred in public areas, on the streets of the city, open to investigation all night long.

So, how does one conduct an investigation into the paranormal at the battlefields around Fredericksburg?

RESEARCH

Legitimate ghost investigators will thoroughly research an area suspected of being haunted: the history, the people who once lived there, the deaths of those involved with the site, any violence associated with the site, and past reports of paranormal events. There are several reasons you want to examine the history of a suspected haunted site.

First, the information can lead to possible explanations of present day hauntings. Second, knowledge of the events and people associated with the site can be a tool to help contact or bring out any residual entities remaining at the site. Third, while a house known for paranormal activity was built within the last few years, the earth upon which it was built may have connections with a sordid and violent past. The houses, themselves, have no history of death or violence, but the ground upon which they were built was once part of some of the bloodiest fighting the world has known. Modern houses virtually carpet the scene of the Union assaults upon the Sunken Road at Fredericksburg; they are built upon the sites of the mass graves dug, then exhumed, in front of Marye's Heights; just off the battlefield roads in the Wilderness are modern houses, built, perhaps, where men, wounded too badly to move, roasted to death; Spotsylvania Court House is seeing development adjacent to the battlefields.

Finally, research will give you names of individuals who owned or were associated with a structure or site. When one is attempting to photograph, or record Electronic Voice Phenomena (EVP), results seem to be better when individuals are addressed by name. For example, some of the best EVP I have ever recorded was at the Jennie Wade Birth House (not the Jennie Wade House where she was shot) on Baltimore Street just north of Breckenridge Street in Gettysburg. (Recalling your history of Gettysburg, you'll remember that Jennie Wade was the only civilian killed in the three-day battle.)

I attribute the success of this particular session to the preliminary research I did on the house. I discovered that a man named John Pfoutz owned the house and that the Wades rented from him at the time of Jennie Wade's birth. Jennie's mother's maiden name was Mary Ann Filby, also discovered during the research process. Jennie's father had been incarcerated by the law, throwing Mrs. Wade and her daughters into virtual poverty. They took over Wade's tailoring business and worked hard sewing to make ends meet. My research gave us something to talk about.

Where does one research the names and events of Fredericksburg that will prove useful in a paranormal investigation?

Fortunately, the Battles of Fredericksburg and Spotsylvania County are some of the most documented events in human history. Volumes have been written about the people living in Spotsylvania County at the time, of the officers and men who fought in the battles, and of the sites, well-known and obscure, where men fought and died. Many of the more readable sources are listed at the end of this book in the "Resources" section. It would be wise to consult these books before doing an investigation at the Fredericksburg and Spotsylvania Battlefields.

The monuments erected upon the battlefields by the men who fought there are historical documents in themselves. Check for names and ranks of the wounded and dead, regimental numbers, and commanders. Use these names to help you establish a connection with those long gone heroes.

Later in this book, in the "Tips for Investigating" sections, you will notice I have included some names of individual people who fought in the haunted areas, names of states from which the regiments came, and some specific things, like nicknames. In other words, I have done some basic historical research for you. Use these names and personal tidbits when you're attempting to photograph remnant spirit energies or gather EVP.

ATTITUDE

This brings us to one of the intangible aspects of "Ghost Hunting." Let us establish the fact that you would personally object to suddenly hearing a voice rudely shouting at you, or calling your name and laughing, or making fun of you as if you were not even there. Would you bother to answer?

Probably not. If entities on "The Other Side" maintain any of their human characteristics and personalities (as most researchers believe) they would still be sensitive to someone barging in on their peace and quiet. This would especially be true of the former denizens of a much more sophisticated, conservative society, such as Victorian America—the Civil War period.

And most importantly, an attitude of respect certainly is due the Civil War soldiers who put their lives on the line—and lost them—here at Fredericksburg and the Spotsylvania County battlefields. Therefore, whenever you enter the "Hallowed Ground" over which they fought and for which they died, whether you are investigating the paranormal or studying the history of the area and the great deeds done here, please conduct yourself with respectfulness.

As my writings about the encampments of reenactors during the anniversary commemorations of the battle and during the filming of the movie "Gettysburg" attest, just as we can see what appear to be spirits of the dead upon occasion, it seems that, as well, they can see us. That is perhaps why so many reenactor encampments teem with stories of "the most authentic-looking reenactor" passing through the camp … then vanishing, or campfires being seen where there was no encampment, only to disappear as inspectors approach. It seems as if the spirits feel more comfortable in the midst of those who look familiar, as they and their friends looked so long ago, before there was a battle at this place called Fredericksburg, before the names Chancellorsville, The Wilderness and Spotsylvania Court House came to represent abject horror and savagery … before they were sent on their one-way journey to eternity.

I have gone into the Triangular Field at Gettysburg armed with a Civil War Drill Manual and a roster of the names of the men who fought there. I have called the men to attention and read off their names and have gotten EVP which sounded like voices answering me, voices that could not be heard while they were being recorded.

Other investigators have tried playing Civil War Era music to "relax" the spirits, make them feel more like they are once again alive in their own time.

I took a tuning fork, registered to the vibration of "om," the universal tone of the earth and all creation according to Eastern religion, and set it vibrating in the Triangular Field. Whether it was the tuning fork, or my calling the men of the 15th Georgia to attention to receive their pay using the Confederate Manual, or reading from their regimental roster the dead and wounded left in the once horrid field, that produced results that night, I'll never know. But they responded, unheard by my ear, recorded for posterity on my digital recorder as a muffled "Yes, sir," and sharp, irritated roars, sounding like angry frustration.

EQUIPMENT

It's very likely that you came to Fredericksburg to visit the battlefields, learn a little history, and relax at one of the fine motels or restaurants in the area. You may even have come to Fredericksburg not realizing that there was a second side to the town and battlefield, a side steeped in the paranormal: the spirit side of the area where 100,000 fell as casualties in four major battles. A paranormal investigation or "ghost hunt" was not even on your agenda until you got here and realized that there are other things to learn in addition to its storied battle history.

Even if you have come unprepared to search for ghosts, you probably brought with you the right equipment to do a basic investigation.

As many paranormal investigators will state, the most important piece of ghost hunting equipment is the investigator himself. The investigator's preliminary research, attitude, adherence to protocol, attention to detail, experience, common sense, and raw intuition are the most potent pieces of equipment in his or her arsenal.

There are some pieces of equipment, however, that can be helpful in first locating paranormal anomalies, then in recording them for later analysis. Therefore, field equipment for a paranormal investigation can generally be divided into two categories: 1) Detecting Equipment and 2) Recording Equipment.

Detecting Equipment

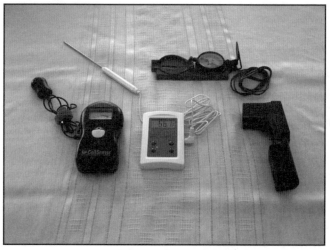

First, let me say that there is no such thing as a "ghost detector." There are, however, instruments that can detect anomalies associated with what appear to be remnant spirit energies. Detecting equipment identifies and locates those particular anomalies.

Detecting equipment will help you know if a particular site is active at the time. This equipment can range from sophisticated Electromagnetic Field Meters to one's own psychic sensitivity.

Investigators have had some success with infrared Thermal Scanners (also known as Non-contact Thermometers or Remote Temperature Sensors). A Thermal Scanner will detect temperature at a distance using infrared light. Historically, persons recalling ghostly encounters mention feeling a chill in the air. A Thermal Scanner can be a good way of locating spirit energies through temperature anomalies. Normally, an investigator will do a 360 degree sweep to see if there are any severe anomalies in the temperature. Where there are large variations in temperature, he'll take a picture. Often the picture will reveal an orb or paranormal mist.

Rick Fisher, renowned ghost hunter and Director of the Pennsylvania Paranormal Society, while doing a sweep of the field of Pickett's Charge at Gettysburg, got readings on his Thermal Scanner as low as minus three degrees, when the ambient temperature was between thirty and thirty-three degrees. When I walked over to investigate the temperature anomalies, I felt the cold. While I stood there others took pictures which showed orbs "gathering" curiously around me. The drawback to Thermal Scanners is that the "beam" they send out to detect temperature broadens the farther away the object sensed is. You cannot really be sure if what you are detecting is directly in front of you, or off to the side a few degrees. If used in a general way outdoors, however, the Thermal Scanner is good enough for finding anomalies.

Indoors, a quick-read thermometer—one that registers a change in temperature within one second—can be helpful. The sensor is taped to a two to three foot wooden dowel so that it cannot inadvertently read the investigator's own body heat. As well, mounting the sensor on a long dowel gives the investigator a little more reach. Paranormal energies—"ghosts"—sometimes roam to the upper corners of rooms.

Using Thermal Scanners and quick-read thermometers also confirm that there is a type of "heat" energy associated with these orbs. Photographs indicate they have some sort of light energy, either generated by themselves or stimulated by the infrared or flash lighting used by cameras. They also may have reflective properties indicating they contain some "real" substance.

Some investigators like to carry Electromagnetic Field (EMF) meters. Many investigators have captured orbs on film or video after a fellow investigator has seen a spike on the EMF meter. Electromagnetism is another attribute of orbs and paranormal mists—what investigators are convinced are the physical manifestations of spirits in our world. Some speculate that this is why the tiny hairs on the back of one's neck or arms stand in the presence of spirit energy. Others point to this electromagnetism, in the form of static electricity, as one of the reasons why dogs and cats are sensitive to ghost phenomena. Their fur reacts to the infinitesimal electromagnetic charge associated with ghosts. Electromagnetism may also account for EVP. It is my theory that electromagnetism is the method spirit entities use to communicate.

As an English major in college, I was required to take a course in linguistics, the study of language. A sub-category of linguistics is Articulatory Phonetics, the study of how speech sounds are produced. Almost invariably, to produce speech, some kind of physical component is needed—lips, tongue, teeth, lungs to expel air through a larynx—all of which have decomposed on a dead person. The only thing that hasn't decomposed is the energy, which, according to the first law of thermodynamics, cannot be created or destroyed, but only changes form. More studies are needed, but electromagnetic energy may be being manipulated in order to communicate with the living. Who is manipulating the energy? The dead.

I have two examples of paranormal electromagnetic communication with the deaf. In the first case, which occurred in June of 2005, a friend was visiting Sachs Bridge, in Gettysburg, with his wife, who is deaf, and her two friends, who are also deaf. Suddenly his wife began signing to him that she was having a paranormal experience. My friend took a picture and an orb appeared in it near her. He asked her what she had experienced. She was astonished and told him she had heard voices. The other fellow was at the far end of the bridge. He came running back to the group and signed that he had heard someone unseen talking at the far end of the bridge.

In the second case, a woman was visiting Sachs Bridge at night with a friend who is deaf. According to her description of the evening, shortly after their arrival he began acting strangely, with a look of serious concentration on his face. He asked her to take a picture, which she did. The photo revealed a faint orb just above his right shoulder, about the level of his ear. He asked her to continue to take pictures as he walked the length of the bridge. Every photo she took had an orb in it, seemingly the same one, hovering near him. Later he described "hearing something" in his hearing aids. He couldn't really describe it except by saying that it sounded like "electricity."

At the far side of the bridge from the parking area, he suddenly became even more intense. He requested another picture and this one showed a large, bright, white orb floating slightly above his head and to his right. After a few minutes in what she described as a semi-trancelike state, he told her that he had been hearing the voice of a woman, or a boy, perhaps a very young soldier. Try as he might, he could not make out what the voice was saying. He decided to try an experiment and removed his hearing aids, without which he can hear nothing. He acknowledged that he was still hearing the same voice as before.

On the pathway that runs along Marsh Creek he continued to hear voices that indicated where they could get pictures of orbs. Finally that night, he heard a voice say "Get out!" They took that as a sign that the investigation was over, and left.

What do these two cases of the deaf hearing voices mean? My interpretation is that the orbs, which appear to have electromagnetic characteristics to them, actually may pass through our bodies (like most electromagnetic waves do) and affect the hearing by direct interface with the auditory nerve. One theory is that a seat of paranormal prescience is the right medial temporal lobe of the brain, which may explain why orbs were photographed near the person's head or on their right side. Could this be the method available to "ghosts" to be able to communicate with us via magnetic tape, digital sound equipment, even clairaudience? When we see a full-body apparition, is it because the "ghost's" electromagnetism has interfaced directly with our optic nerve? More experimentation and research is needed along these lines.

EMF meters are readily available through scientific equipment catalogues or on the internet. Some have several sensitivity settings; some are multi-field; some have audible alarms whenever an electromagnetic field is detected. As with the sensor on the quick-read thermometer, it is a good idea to tape the sensor of the EMF meter to a dowel to keep it away from the investigator's own electromagnetic field.

I have placed the sensor against my chest and set off the EMF meter. As I've stated before, we are electric beings: our brains generate electrical energy. When we die, some biologists have recorded a "light shout"—photons exploding from our bodies at the moment of death. One of the theories for an area being haunted is that perhaps this burst of energy is somehow captured in the environment—by quartz in the granite stones located in geologic formations on battlefields or used as foundations in older houses—and then replayed like a recording under certain, special conditions. It is just one more theory...

If the cost of an EMF meter is prohibitive, a compass may be used to detect magnetism in an area. When the compass spins, you may be in the realm of influence of a spirit. I once saw a small bar magnet mounted on a gimbal so it would rotate toward whatever axis to which it was attracted. The only problem with compasses or magnets is that they have no audible warning and so must be watched to detect any anomalies.

CAUTION: A sensitive EMF meter can be set off by exactly what they are supposed to read: electromagnetic fields given off by computers, televisions, microwave ovens, reading lamps, household electrical wires and cellphones. Make sure you are aware of other fields near where you are using the meter to prevent false readings. Turn off your cellphone or leave it in your car during an investigation. Even compasses can be thrown off by ambient electromagnetic waves.

Recording Equipment

The study of the paranormal is by nature controversial. Sighting ghosts, hearing phantom footsteps, smelling the perfume of a long dead woman from a by-gone era, usually meant one was immediately classified as delusional. While history is filled with accounts of ghost encounters, they have almost always officially been relegated to fiction and the imagination.

But therein lies the problem. History *is* filled with accounts of paranormal phenomena. Virtually every generation from every nation and tribe and society throughout history has its stories of the dead re-visiting the living. They may all have different reasons for the visitation, but they are still accounts of the dead coming back. Are that many people throughout history delusional? It is highly doubtful.

Until just recently, we had to take the word of the individual as to what they had experienced as proof of the paranormal event. That is why equipment to record the event to analyze later or show proof to others has become essential.

Today, with some basic modern equipment, we can capture evidence of the paranormal. You probably already have this equipment: A camera and an audio recorder.

What ghost hunters call "orbs" or "ectoplasm," "paranormal mist" or "vortexes" are, in their opinion, the evidence of spirit activity. Usually they cannot be seen by the human eye. Some theorize that spirit energy is in a wavelength impossible to see with the human eye (although some psychics and other highly sensitive people claim they can see orbs or ectoplasm with the naked eye). However, the shutter of a camera works so quickly that, if spirit activity is present, it can be captured.

Cameras

Many researchers like to use a digital camera because it gives them immediate results. Digital cameras are also nice because you can record almost an infinite number of shots by deleting those showing no evidence of paranormal activity. Images from digital cameras can be easily downloaded to computers and shared with others, enlarged or "enhanced" and studied more closely, which is a good reason not to delete any shots from your camera until you've had a chance to examine them on a larger computer screen.

Standard cameras, from expensive 35mm types to disposable cameras, have all yielded results when the conditions were right. The only drawback is that you have to wait—sometimes several days, sometimes only an hour—to see the print. The result is that since you are "photographing blind" you don't know if an area is active while you are there.

In other words, for your first time "ghost hunting," the camera you brought with you is fine.

Often, you don't even have to aim the camera at a specific site. Random shots—"from the hip" so to speak—often produce good results. Rick Fisher uses a "sixth sense" to tell him when to snap a photo: he'll get a feeling, intuitively turn a certain way, snap a picture and come up with a photo containing orbs or paranormal mist. Sometimes just turning around and snapping a picture will render a successful "orb" photo, since they seem to follow people as if curious.

Investigating inside a building, we have found that after the investigators have set up equipment, then leave the room, there is a flurry of paranormal activity. It is as if the researchers frighten the entities (which are apparently shy) into retreating, then once the researchers are gone, the entities return to see what was going on.

The point is, don't be afraid to use your own creativity and sensitivity when photographing in a suspected active area.

Video Cameras

Some of the country's most respected paranormal investigators will videotape their entire session. If any paranormal events do occur, the video can be reviewed to show that no hoax was involved. I always videotape my investigations, sometimes using two video cameras—one hand-held and the other one on a tripod—to intercept accusations that things were staged. In addition, you just never know when the video camera, which is running all the time, will pick up something when your still camera is at rest.

Sony makes a camcorder with NightShot®. Canon has its "Super Night Shooting Mode," and Panasonic its MagicVu™. They all give you the opportunity to make videos in complete darkness with infrared lighting. Some even come with an infrared add-on light to extend the range. I have seen them capture "orbs"—and, in an extremely rare case, EVP and orbs—in motion.

Many people think that ghosts only "come out" at night. Once again, a myth perpetuated by Hollywood to exploit the fear factor in all of us. Of the over 1,000 stories of hauntings I have collected, about 45 percent have been reported to have occurred during the daylight hours. Armed with this information, and angered that the National Park at Gettysburg changed its hours for visiting the battlefield as a slap at paranormal investigators, Scott Crownover of the Ghost Research Foundation decided to research photographing entities during the daylight hours. His results, and the results of others using his technique, have been nothing less than astounding. Scott has agreed to share the details of his amazing research for the first time in print.

THE CROWNOVER TECHNIQUE—DIGITAL INFRARED PHOTOGRAPHY
By Scott A. Crownover

It has long been speculated that if ghosts do manifest, they do so slightly within the infrared spectrum. This is a possibility considering that infrared is a longer wavelength of the electromagnetic spectrum and requires less energy than light that is visible to our eyes.

Our eyes can "see" a spectrum of electromagnetic energy from about 400 nanometers to about 700+ nanometers. This is visible light. Infrared extends

---

past this. Near infrared is what we are working with. It ranges from just over 700 nanometers to past 1500 nanometers.

We sometimes get orbs of light in our photographs that are not visible to our eyes when the photo is taken. Many of these can be explained away as dust or moisture, but a few may not be dust or moisture. If we can't see them, then why do they show up on our photos? This is possibly due to the fact that film and digital cameras can "see" longer into the infrared spectrum than the human eye can. This is easy to prove with a digital camera. Point any remote control from a TV or VCR toward the lens of the camera. Push any button on the remote, and if you see a light in the view screen, your camera is sensitive to the near infrared spectrum.

If the supposition were true that some of these orbs are visible in the infrared spectrum, then it would stand to reason that infrared photography would be useful in capturing images of full-bodied apparitions. While there is no hard and fast data to prove this, it would stand to reason that this is an area for exploration.

Infrared photography, however, is fraught with problems. Infrared film is expensive. I have found it on the Internet for $11.49-$11.99 per 36 exposure roll. There is no guarantee that it will be in good condition when it arrives. It is difficult to handle, as it must be kept cool at all times. It must be loaded and unloaded in complete darkness. In addition, much experimentation is necessary to find what works best in your camera. Unless you have your own darkroom, finding a lab that will develop it is very difficult.

All of this was running through my mind as I considered the dilemma of how to use infrared photography in our work as paranormal investigators. I was further frustrated by the fact that one of my favorite sites, the Gettysburg National Military Park, is restricted for nighttime photography, and most investigators take their photos at night. At Gettysburg, this leaves only about an hour of darkness during the summer and slightly more during the off-season.

Most investigators use infrared cameras such as a Sony NightShot® to film at night. They can shoot infrared video and poor quality infrared stills with this camera, but what about day video and higher quality infrared shots? We see moving orbs at night on the video cameras that we use because the NightShot® is specifically designed to record in infrared when switched to the NightShot® mode. Again, there are many explanations for these orbs and you are entitled to your own opinion. But, how do we film this phenomenon during the day? Those images were still only possible with the use of standard infrared film, or were they?

My thought was that, if a digital camera is infrared sensitive, I could possibly block out the visible light and leave only infrared. I looked at literally hundreds of web sites on photography and discovered that it is possible to take infrared photos in daylight without having to buy and process expensive infrared film. The solution seemed simple: use an infrared filter on a digital camera. Digital cameras use CCDs, or charged couple devices to record the image instead of film. They are sensitive to the infrared spectrum. If you place an infrared filter such as a Wratten 87B or Hoya R72 on the camera, you can filter out most visible light. By doing this, you are now able to take infrared photos in broad daylight.

There are some drawbacks to this system, however. With digital still infrared photography, you need bright sunlight and a tripod. The filter (I use a Hoya R72) requires a time exposure of ½ to 1 second. This is too long for taking a freehand photo. If your camera does not support the threads on the filter, simply use plumber's Teflon® tape to secure the filter in front of the lens. It will not leave any adhesive residue when it is removed.

In addition to placing the camera on a tripod, it is necessary to take multiple photos from the same angle in order to compare them with others in the series. It is also imperative to have at least one other person with you while you are taking photographs. That way, there is verification that no one was in the frame when the photo was taken. Because of the technique, anyone in your frame, even at a distance, will be visible. Anyone moving in the distance will appear as a blur. This is where multiple observers are a great asset to the session.

If you set a video camera next to your still camera, you can have a record of everything that transpired during your photography session. This will also serve as verification of the events in front of the camera.

Courtesy of Scott A. Crownover

Devil's Den IR2 Photo

The first person outside of the Ghost Research Foundation to evaluate this new technique was Mark Nesbitt. Mark is an author, historian, paranormal investigator and the foremost authority on the history and hauntings in Gettysburg. I had taken a photo at Devil's Den in Gettysburg that showed two apparitions that were not visible in the frame at the time the photo was taken.

I have not been the only person to use this technique successfully. Craig Rupp took a photograph on Little Round Top that shows an apparition looking over the rock that is home to General Warren's statue. A comparison photograph taken later, shows that the ground is currently too high to reproduce a similar effect.

Courtesy of Craig Rupp

Apparition on Little Round Top

Still cameras are not the only way to work with infrared in the daylight. There are filters available for video cameras as well. Most video cameras will accept a threaded filter. I personally use a Sony TRV-480 with an M&K 1000 filter. This allows me to use the NightShot® feature in broad daylight without damage to the camera.

Using infrared filters now gives paranormal investigators the ability to conduct investigations during the day at sites that are normally inaccessible at night. Once more, as investigators start using these methods, I believe we will see some surprising results.

I do believe that as researchers, if we share our knowledge, the field will definitely benefit from it. Of course, as with any new methodology, more use and testing will be required to see what the full capabilities are.

To view some of the photographs that we at the Ghost Research Foundation have taken, visit our web site at www.ghostsrus.com.

The majority of all ghost encounters are auditory in nature. Along with footsteps, music, and battle noises, some witnesses at Fredericksburg claim to have heard voices: orders being shouted, moans of the wounded, names whispered in their ears, and babies crying.

Attempts at communicating with the dead are not new. Grief-stricken mourners will attempt to talk to the immediately deceased, not believing they could have died; people will speak at gravesites to long dead relatives as a self-comforting measure; over the centuries, individuals have recruited psychics—some legitimate, some bogus—to help them talk to dead loved ones. An entire "industry"— Spiritualism—grew in the 19th Century out of relatives' desire to communicate with the generation slaughtered during the Civil War. Renowned inventors Thomas Edison and Guglielmo Marconi worked on machines to attempt to communicate with the dead.

Some of the first EVP was recorded in 1959 on regular reel-to-reel magnetic tape by Friedrich Jurgenson who, while recording bird songs alone in an open field, inadvertently recorded a male voice expertly discussing, in Norwegian, nocturnal bird songs. Repeated experiments produced more voices recorded on the tape, although unheard by Jurgenson while he was recording. Eventually he ruled out extraneous sources such as radio or television broadcasts—the voices relayed personal information and even began giving Jurgenson instructions on how to more effectively record the bird songs! A Latvian researcher named Konstantin Raudive worked with Jurgenson and eventually recorded over 100,000 voices, finally publishing his results in 1971 in his book *Breakthrough.*

In 2006 I had the distinct pleasure of meeting and interviewing Sarah Estep, the woman who founded the American Association of EVP. She explained how, after hearing that the voices of the dead could be recorded, she set out on her life-changing quest to communicate with the Other World. She promised herself to give the experiment seven days: if she received no EVP after a week, she would quit. For four days—two hours in the morning and two at night—she would ask if anyone was there and would they answer. Four days went by with nothing on the tape but Sarah's own voice. Finally, on the evening of the fourth day, she was bored with asking the same old questions. Apparently, the dead were bored, too, for when she asked, "What is it like where you are?" She got the response, "Beauty." Several hundred thousand recordings later, and Sarah has been able to classify EVP: Class A is the best, easily understood; Class B needs some hard listening and perhaps some acoustical clean-up to understand; Class C is merely garble, roars, clicks, and whistles.

There are several techniques for recording EVP. The site is important: battlefields, graveyards or buildings with a haunted past are more likely sources of EVP. One technique is to start a tape running and simply walk away. Reviewing the entire tape will reveal if any extraneous voices were recorded. Shelly Sykes, co-author of the series *The Gettysburg Ghost Gang*, uses this technique with a compact cassette tape recorder with remarkable success.

It is important to always use a new tape so that previously recorded information won't "bleed" through. You may also want to employ a witness to, or videotape, the unwrapping of the tape, so no one can cry "fraud." Some investigators insist that you use a remote microphone as well, since many reel-to-reel cassette tape recorders' motors make noise that may be mistaken for EVP.

Another technique is to ask questions into the recorder, then pause for answers. Some of the most remarkable—and somewhat disturbing—experiments I have done were with a digital credit-card sized Panasonic Model No. RR-DR60. The recorder is set on voice activation mode. I ask a question and the recorder's LED light glows steadily to indicate something is being recorded. While I ask the question, the electronic numbers in the display roll forward to show recording is taking place. When I stop talking the light flashes on and off (to indicate that it is in voice activation mode but not recording anything) and the numbers cease to roll. I pause for thirty to fifty seconds. Suddenly, in total silence, the light begins to glow steadily and the numbers begin to roll. The seemingly impossible is taking place—*something is being recorded that cannot be heard.*

Upon playback, various qualities of noises can be heard. Sometimes there is just a loud (extremely loud!) roar, as if something were very angry or, more to the point, frustrated. It is guttural, explosive, and can be painful to the ears if the recorder is held too close. Other sounds are background noises, like the "white noise" heard during a party: a sort of murmur, a mixing of voices, indistinguishable as individual voices or phrases, but a low mumbling behind everything. While these sounds are not understandable as words or sentences, they are still remarkable, because they are noises recorded in complete silence! There should be nothing on the recorder since there was nothing to be heard during the recording.

Although leaving a recorder without monitoring it is not recommended (anyone could leave a "message"), I set a new Panasonic digital recorder on its "voice-activated" setting on a twelve-foot thick, brick casement sill at Fort Delaware. No one was around, and yet, for 18 seconds the recorder captured strange, muffled sounds out of time.

Another time, I left my Panasonic overnight in the oldest room of the *Ghosts of Gettysburg Candlelight Walking Tour®* Headquarters. It was a snowy winter night and the building had been closed for over a month. The next morning I realized that, starting at 3:58 A.M., the recorder started recording and captured 40 minutes of EVP.

CAUTION: Respect others already engaged in an investigation. When someone is trying to get EVP, be quiet. If you are trying to get EVP and someone talks or coughs, identify it on the recorder so it won't be confused with legitimate EVP. Force yourself to pause 6, 7, or 8 breaths before asking another question. Have patience.

Do not be discouraged if you are not one of those sensitive enough to pick up on the paranormal world. Many people have visited Fredericksburg scores of times—many have lived here all their lives—and never had a paranormal experience.

The answer to why some of us experience the paranormal and others do not, is because we are all born with natural differences in perception. Psychic abilities, or even just sensitivity to psychic happenings, are dissimilar in all of us. Some of us have better hearing than others; some better eyesight, or a better singing voice. Just like all our senses, some are born with a more acute sensitivity to the paranormal. The customers on our tours are a good example: No one is smoking on the tour or in the area. Suddenly, one smells old-fashioned pipe tobacco burning and someone standing right next to them does not. That may be an indication that one is more sensitive to a paranormal event than another.

The best part is that many experts agree that one can develop one's psychic sensitivities.

But the fact that someone has never had a paranormal experience in their life until they get to the Fredericksburg Battlefields, is indication of only one thing: it is the *place* that contains the spirits they can experience.

THE BATTLE OF FREDERICKSBURG

"Antietam was nothing to it."
Capt. John Lathrop, 35th Massachusetts Infantry

The Battle of Fredericksburg, within the span of two days, illustrated decisively the futility of military tactics of the past, and the innovation and future horror of military tactics to come. It showed the importance of logistics and planning, and how the blunderings of an awkward military bureaucracy can bog down a campaign and decide, weeks before the fighting, the outcome of the battle. It also displayed, once again, the indomitable courage of the American soldier.

The Battle of Fredericksburg can be divided into three general phases. Chronologically they were: 1) The crossing of the Rappahannock River by the Union and defense of the riverbank by Confederates on December 11; 2) The December 13 attacks upon "Stonewall" Jackson's Confederate Corps on the southern end of the field; and 3) The Union assaults against the Sunken Road below Marye's Heights later that day.

PRELUDE TO BATTLE

On November 7, 1862, the command of the Federal Army of the Potomac was transferred from Major General George B. McClellan to Major General Ambrose E. Burnside. Within three days, the new Union commander presented a plan of battle to the government, which delayed their approval until November 14. The whole plan depended upon Burnside getting his army of 120,000 quickly across the Rappahannock River at Fredericksburg in order to strike south towards Richmond, the capital of the Confederacy. Since Confederates had burned all the bridges across the Rappahannock, Burnside needed portable pontoon bridges to arrive at Fredericksburg precisely when his army did, before Confederate General Robert E. Lee could ascertain the Federals' intentions and oppose the crossing.

Delay and bureaucratic foul-ups were the hallmarks of the Federals preceding the battle. The first of the Federals' "Grand Divisions" arrived across the Rappahannock from Fredericksburg in the afternoon of November 17. The pontoon bridges, however, had not. Lee was now tipped off as to where the Yankees were headed and began to concentrate his army—which would eventually number 78,000—at Fredericksburg.

The bridges finally arrived November 25. After considering a river crossing downstream from Fredericksburg at Skinker's Neck, Burnside announced to his generals that they would cross at Fredericksburg. Shortly after moonset, around 1:00 A.M., December 11, 1862, engineers from the Federal Army of the Potomac began wrangling the cumbersome pontoon boats down the slope from "Chatham," the 18th Century mansion on Stafford Heights, to the edge of the river. Under the cover of darkness and fog on the river, the engineers got the bridges built about halfway across.

Example of Pontoon Boat on Display at Chatham

Confederates from Brigadier General William Barksdale's Mississippi Brigade, waited in rifle pits and riverfront dwellings and listened to the sounds of construction echoing through the misty night. Barksdale had determined, once he had informed General Lee of the enemy's intentions of bridging the river at Fredericksburg, to delay their crossing for as long as he could so that Lee could gather his forces together.

Out on the unfinished bridges, the unarmed engineers and construction troops heard the bell in the clock tower of Saint George's Episcopal Church—one of the landmarks of the Fredericksburg skyline—toll 5:00 A.M. Through the rising mist, one of the Union officers saw a line of human arms flailing up and down: the unmistakable motion of men ramming home charges in muzzle-loading weapons. A few minutes later, an engineer on the end of one of the bridges heard an ominous shout through the fog: "Fire!" and bullets ripped into the wood of the bridges and tore through the flesh of the men. Union soldiers collapsed upon the unfinished bridge or tumbled, helpless, into the icy river. Those who could, fled back in panic to the shore, but there was no safety there. For the rifled-musket of the Civil War, the opposite bank of the Rappahannock was easily within range, and men, mules and horses went down.

Virtually the same thing was happening at the middle pontoon bridge site, across from the city boat landing. Confederates rushed down the old ferry access, "Rocky Lane" to the end of the docks and fired into the engineers on the bridges already two thirds across. Work on that bridge ended as the Federals ran for their lives back to the river bank.

The Union commanders decided that the Confederates must be routed by artillery, and began a bombardment of the town. By 10:00 A.M., 183 Federal cannons were firing and Fredericksburg was being blasted to pieces. When the gunners were satisfied they had done their job, the engineers returned to the bridges. Just as they began to work, the Mississippians emerged from the rubble and started picking them off again. This sequence repeated itself several times throughout the morning.

Meantime, a pontoon bridge a mile downstream at the "Lower Crossing" was completed, but General Burnside refused to allow his troops to cross until the upstream bridges were complete for fear they would be isolated without support and cut to pieces.

At the Upper and Middle Crossings, work was still stymied by the persistent rebel sharpshooters. At 12:30 P.M. Burnside ordered all available Union cannons to fire on the town, and for an hour they again pulverized Fredericksburg. In all, some 8,000 shells had rained down on the city. Brick buildings suffered, but the shells merely passed through the wooden structures leaving holes that occupying Confederates used to fire through. Sophia Street, closest to the river, looked like it had been plowed and virtually every window in the city had been broken out.

Middle Pontoon Crossing

Burnside's detailed plans, established some five weeks before, were crumbling before his eyes, with his entire army held up by a handful of obstinate rebel riflemen. At that moment, Brigadier General Henry Hunt, Burnside's artillery chief, passed on an idea that one of the engineers had suggested: ferry a few infantrymen across in the pontoon boats to drive the pesky Confederates back away from the river so the engineers could finish the bridges.

Burnside hesitated. Something like that had never been done before in the history of the U. S. Army. Could it be successful, or would Burnside be merely sentencing the men to their own execution in the middle of the river? Burnside wanted only volunteers.

Colonel Norman J. Hall's 7th Michigan, when asked if they would cross the river in boats to drive out the enemy, responded with three cheers.

It would be eight decades before the United States Marines would bring into the common military lexicon, "amphibious assault." The precursor of all of them was about to begin on the Rappahannock River at Fredericksburg. Just like the waterborne attacks of World War II, this one was also preceded by a massive artillery bombardment beginning at 3:00 P.M. When the fire slackened, the boats would shove off.

After a half hour, the big guns fell silent and the assault troops of the 7th Michigan rushed to the boats. They had scarcely loaded when the Confederates opened on them again. Under orders not to return fire but to concentrate on paddling or poling across, the men were helpless. The boats took terrific fire until they were two-thirds of the way across, then a curious thing happened. The Confederate fire slowed to a trickle. The steep riverbank below Sophia Street hid the assault craft from the Confederates and the landing was made.

The landing party rushed up the slope to Sophia Street and began surrounding the houses where the rebels hid. They had been given the order, "No quarter"—take no prisoners. While some disobeyed the order, others rushed into houses and shot or bayoneted every man inside. In less than a half hour, Sophia Street was cleared.

But the Confederates were not about to retire without a fight, and the battle took on a character that would become the bloody hallmark of wars of the next century-and-a-half. From the Spanish American War through the fighting after D-Day in Normandy to Fallujah, a new type of tactical fighting needed to be learned by warriors—house-to-house, urban street fighting—and it began in Fredericksburg.

Confederates defended the town from the alleys and backyards behind Sophia Street, but the 7th Michigan was buying time for the engineers to complete the bridges. Massachusetts troops were ferried across to bolster the Wolverine's position and as the bridges were completed, they were ordered to advance beyond the waterfront and push the rebels out of the town to make room for more Union solders to land via the bridges.

Federals muscled their way up Hawke Street, taking awful casualties at the intersection of Hawke and Caroline; the 20th Massachusetts lost 97 men in and around the intersection. Night fell early in December, and still the fighting went on. Backyards became battlegrounds and dooryards deathtraps. One Federal broke into a second floor room and was shot through the window by a Confederate across the street. The fighting was illuminated by musket flashes. Men were wounded by splinters flying from brick chimneys and wooden framing. The horror of not knowing from which window or doorway the next shot would come was demoralizing. Finally, with the groans of the wounded echoing through the darkened street, the lack of light brought an end to the carnage. By 7:00 P.M. most of the firing died down and Confederates began retreating from the town.

Hawke Street Looking Towards Caroline Street

With Confederate resistance quelled, December 12 was spent marching Union forces across the Rappahannock and into the city. Communication on a battlefield is primary, and often the difference between victory and defeat. Burnside ordered his chief signal officer to run a telegraph line from occupied Fredericksburg across the lower and upper pontoon bridges to connect headquarters with the far left flank of the army. The communicating device was a clever magnetic "pointer" system: dial a letter on the sending device and the pointer spins to the same letter on the receiver. It was claimed to be the first time the magnetic telegraph was used upon the battlefield.

Federals drained five feet of freezing water from a canal that crossed what would be the battlefield west of the city. They also began looting.

Wanton, illogical destruction began in what had once been one of the finer cities of the South—the boyhood home of George Washington and residence of his mother, Mary. Private homes were vandalized, fine arts destroyed, libraries sacked, personal treasures stolen, and businesses ransacked beyond anything that had happened in the war previously. Normally, 19th Century war was not waged upon civilians; at Fredericksburg, all that turned around.

DECEMBER 13—A DAY OF SLAUGHTER

Most visitors to Fredericksburg arrive at the National Park Service's Visitor Center, see the exhibits, explore the famous Sunken Road behind it, and assume their visit to the battlefield is over. They are wrong. Some of the fiercest fighting took place just a few miles south of the Sunken Road and stone wall, along the Fredericksburg and Potomac Railroad.

The first Federal assaults were planned at dawn on December 13, 1862. Northern forces under Major General William B. Franklin (one of Burnside's three "Grand Divisions" into which he divided his army) were to launch the attacks from the Bowling Green Road, across the Fredericksburg and Potomac Railroad to strike Confederates under Thomas J. "Stonewall" Jackson near Prospect Hill. Franklin used Major General George G. Meade's division and Brigadier General John Gibbon's division, totaling about 8,500 men, for the assault.[1]

The morning dawned gray and misty. The Union assault, which was to get off early, had been delayed. It was nearing 10:00 A.M., and the fog was just beginning to rise. Like ghosts, the Union troops moved out of the haze from the Bowling Green Road and headed toward the railroad. Suddenly, there were muffled artillery discharges from their left and rear. Major John Pelham, the 24-year-old commander of J. E. B. Stuart's Horse Artillery, had used the fog to gain an advantageous position and raked the Union line, halting its advance. Ordered to retire from the exposed position, he refused, and fought under serious counter-battery fire from the Federals, until his ammunition was gone. He drew the admiration of General Lee himself who commented, "It is glorious to see such courage in one so young."[2] "Stonewall" Jackson asked Stuart, "Have you another Pelham, General? If so, I wish you would give him to me!"[3]

Pelham, with one gun, had managed to hold up the entire Union assault for an hour. After Pelham withdrew, Meade continued his advance. Jackson's men waited patiently until the Federals were within 500 yards of a forested hill hiding 14 cannons, then opened fire. Gaps opened in the Federal ranks, and Union soldiers dropped into whatever depressions they could find near the railroad and in the open fields beyond.

Jackson's guns drew artillery fire from the Northerners and there ensued an hour-long artillery duel. So many artillery horses were shot down that the rebels re-named the place, "Dead-horse Hill."

When the Confederate artillery fire died down, Meade's men continued their advance and struck a 600 yard gap in Jackson's line inadvertently left unguarded. In their drive through the Confederate line they ran into a brigade of South Carolinians. Confederate Brigadier General Maxcy Gregg mistook the Yankees for retreating Southerners and withheld his fire. It cost him his life. He was shot in the spine and died later.

Though Jackson had left a space in his line, he had arranged his reserves in column and during the breakthrough launched them into the fought-out Union spearhead. The massive Confederate counterattack pushed Meade's men all the way back across the railroad and back to the Bowling Green Road. Once the Confederates got in range, they were stopped by the massed Union artillery.

Federals and Confederates tried additional assaults in the late afternoon, but both failed. The carnage at one point in the lines was so terrible, it was christened "The Slaughter Pen."[4]

Burnside's plan was to wait for success on the southern end of the field, then launch assaults upon the Confederates at Marye's Heights, just to the west of the city of Fredericksburg. Never one to believe much in his own plans, however, Burnside ordered the Grand Division of Major General Edwin V. Sumner to advance against Longstreet's Confederates.

Just before noon Union infantry lined up shoulder-to-shoulder, emerged from the streets of the city, and began crossing the open fields to the west. Almost simultaneously, Confederate artillery from atop Marye's Heights began lobbing shells into their packed ranks. Men remembered seeing arms, hands, legs and clothing flying into the air above their heads, the hideous result of artillery fire upon massed ranks of infantry.[5]

In front of the Union troops lay the millrace, fifteen feet across and five feet deep, partially filled with freezing water. The only places to cross it were at bridges over three streets leading out of town. These quickly became bottlenecks as Confederate skirmishers, upon their retreat, removed the floors of the bridges leaving just the "stringers" for hundreds of Union troops to attempt to cross. Once across the millrace, the Northerners had to re-aligned their ranks and push on. The last impediment to the Union assault was a wide open field known as the Fair Grounds which was swept by Confederate rifle fire from a virtually unseen enemy standing behind a chin-high stone wall in a sunken road.

Assault after assault repeated the same horrifying and deadly routine. Some of the surviving Union troops found shelter behind the few fence posts left around the Fair Grounds. Other sought relief behind the few buildings in the area: a brick grocery building called Sisson's Store; a house and wheelwright shop owned by the Stratton family. Men and officers piled up behind these structures, like flotsam in the lee of an island during a storm. Throughout the afternoon and into the evening the futile assaults continued. Fifteen Union brigades tried to pierce the Confederate line. They pressed on through "heaps of dead and wounded."[6] Men were cut in two by shells, entrails flying in all directions. They were decapitated, and slumped, some still kneeling, headless, clinging to their muskets. Unbelievably, one man was seen running past an advancing column, without a head, until he tumbled into the millrace.[7] One Confederate saw around the Stratton House that the dead were so thick you could walk on them. Union troops holding their fire as they advanced only made the slaughter easier for Confederates; one wrote afterward, "Blood and brains were scattered everywhere."[8] One man was still alive after a shell gutted him and set fire to his clothing; those who passed saw that the form sizzled and convulsed, probably still alive as he slowly roasted.[9] Soldiers' leather-soled shoes slipped on the grass because there was so much blood; "None would believe men could bleed so much," a Union soldier remembered. "Barrels of blood had apparently been poured on the ground...."[10] Toward the end, the fallen wounded clutched at the legs of the fresh units trying to stop their comrades from a certain death.

Wall at the Sunken Road

The "butcher's bill," as the soldiers called the casualty list, was appalling. In one hour full of horror the Union army lost 4,000 men. All totaled, Burnside lost 12,600 in killed, wounded and missing, with some 8,400 casualties occurring before the stone wall and sunken road. Lee lost about 5,300.

INVESTIGATING THE FREDERICKSBURG BATTLEFIELD

Many sites on property owned by the National Park Service can be considered haunted, but due to Park Service regulations, a full-scale paranormal investigation is prohibited. You may, however, go discretely to certain areas on the Park and conduct your own, small-scale investigation. (When I say "small scale investigation" I mean two people.) As a matter of fact, these smaller investigations often yield great results. Please obey park regulations and leave areas which are closed at dusk.

Fortunately for paranormalists, much of the Battle of Fredericksburg, like the Battle of Gettysburg, was fought in the town itself, on public streets, in public areas which still remain accessible. This opens a number of places for investigations, but also provides some challenges.

In any paranormal investigation private homes and yards are off limits. However, because of the nature of the fighting and historical activity in the very streets of Fredericksburg, public sidewalks, streets, alleys and parks near an alleged haunted site may yield as much evidence as the building itself.

Some of the sites mentioned in this book have no ghost story associated with them—as of now! You, as an investigator, have an opportunity to discover whatever remnants the once-living left behind. While investigating these sites, keep all your senses piqued; expect the unexpected; prepare to witness and document a ghost encounter. Perhaps, *you* will help to add to the haunted history of Fredericksburg.

And it seems that we *do* leave something of us behind after death under certain circumstances. Areas that tend to be haunted are scenes of conflict, battle, and death, where emotional energy was being expended at an all-time high; hospital sites, where men are fighting for their lives and have the time to think about their families and friends they will leave behind; and burial sites, which include individual graves, mass gravesites and former burial sites where bodies have been removed.

NOTE: Directions to all haunted sites begin from the Fredericksburg Visitor Center at the corner of Caroline and Charlotte Streets.

Chronologically, the first scenes of conflict during the Battle of Fredericksburg occurred on December 11, 1862, near the banks of the Rappahannock River. Keep in mind that these are just some of the places of intense fighting in and around the city of Fredericksburg. As your research of the battles continues and your knowledge increases, you will certainly find other sites that are worthy of investigation.

Upper Pontoon Crossing Site

Upper Pontoon Crossing and Michigan Monument

On that foggy morning of December 11, 1862, as Union engineers began constructing pontoon bridges for the army to cross the Rappahannock, Confederate riflemen, alerted by the sounds, waited for them along the west bank of the river. The fog lifted and rebel rifles spoke. Soon, the Rappahannock was stained with the blood of the bridge builders. Continued construction of the bridges, even after the city was shelled, was impossible: the Mississippians had taken refuge in the houses and rubble along Sophia Street and would not be dislodged. Finally, an amphibious assault—soldiers in boats—was launched at the site of the Upper Pontoon Bridge Crossing at the foot of Hawke Street. It succeeded in driving the Confederates away from the river, but they lodged themselves in other houses farther up Hawke, on Caroline and Princess Anne Streets, firing at the advancing Federals from windows and doorways.

How to Get There

From the Visitor Center, go east (downhill) on Charlotte Street to Sophia Street. Turn left and follow Sophia seven blocks to Hawke Street. Park near the monuments to the men of the 7th Michigan Infantry.

CAUTION: The Rappahannock River is at the bottom of the hill. A misstep could place you in the river. Therefore, it is NOT recommended that you investigate too close to the river at night. The area is not widely visited, so daylight might yield some fine EVP as well as photos using the Crownover Technique.

Tips on Investigating

The area is along a public street and is open all night. The first troops to cross in the boats were from the 7th Michigan. Lieutenant Colonel Henry Baxter of the 7th was shot through the lung while crossing with the regiment. He was replaced by Major Thomas Hunt. The 17th Mississippi under Colonel John Fiser virtually went toe-to-toe with the Michigan troops. For EVP work, try addressing these two units: ask them about their commanders, or about the helpless feeling they must have had crossing in the boats.

Fredericksburg had several civilians killed during the fighting. One such casualty occurred near the corner of Sophia and Hawke Streets. Captain George Macy of the 20th Massachusetts was given an elderly citizen of Fredericksburg as a guide by his commander. The man was understandably reluctant to do any "point duty" for the Federals with Mississippi bullets flying at them. At the corner the guide balked, but Lacy pushed him out into the street where he was promptly shot dead, mistaken by the sharpshooting Rebels for a Yankee. At least three other adult civilian deaths appear to have occurred between December 11 and 13. There is also one report of three children being killed by one shell.[1]

Hawke and Caroline Streets

Confederates contested virtually every back yard between Sophia and Caroline Street while the pontoon bridges were finished and reinforcements came across the river. The 19th Massachusetts crossed the river and reinforced the 7th Michigan on the right. Street fighting ensued. Federals took refuge in a blind alley, which still exists, off Hawke Street; more crammed behind the houses. As Yankees tried to advance through the yards to Caroline Street, Rebels would blast them with volleys at nearly point-blank range. According to Historian Frank O'Reilly, the intersection of Hawke and Caroline Street filled with over 100 dead and wounded Union soldiers, all shot down by Confederates ensconced in the houses along Caroline Street. It became one of the bloodiest examples of street fighting in American History. It is no wonder that Caroline Street hosts so many spirit entities from the Civil War.

How to Get There

From the Visitor Center, go east (downhill) on Charlotte Street to Sophia Street. Turn left and follow Sophia seven blocks to Hawke Street. Park near the monuments to the men of the 7th Michigan Infantry and walk up Hawke Street.

Tips on Investigating

Many sites fought over during the American Civil War have been obscured by modern development. Fortunately, Fredericksburg has clung tenaciously to its heritage: of the 500 or so houses that were here during the battle, some 300 still stand—more than in Gettysburg; more even than in Williamsburg. The best part about investigating the remnant spirits of the fighting is that Hawke Street and Caroline Street still intersect at the same spot they did when the armies clashed there. It is easy to visualize the battle along Hawke Street from Sophia to Caroline: the blind alley is to the left halfway up the street and can be used as a landmark.

Alley Off of Hawke Street

The area is open to the public after dark. Use common sense, however, and respect the property-owners' rights when doing an investigation. Hawke Street is relatively quiet and could yield EVP. In addition to the units mentioned above, other units that participated in the street fighting were from the Philadelphia Brigade, including the 106th and 72nd Pennsylvania. The 42nd and 59th New York regiments also fought in the streets before you. One individual tragedy occurred in the vicinity. Michael Redding of the 19th Massachusetts went down after the regiment was driven back towards the river from Caroline Street. His comrades attempted to evacuate him but he shooed them away, secure in the knowledge they would return. When they finally did, they found Redding dead, bayoneted at least seven times, some thought in retaliation for one Union commander's order to "bayonet every armed man firing from a house."[2]

The Millrace (Kenmore Avenue)

As the Union attacks emerged from the west side of the city of Fredericksburg on December 13, 1862, before they could reach the open fields that led to the Sunken Road, they struck a ditch, partially filled with water that was used as a runoff sluiceway for the canal north of the city. It was five feet deep and a formidable fifteen feet wide. Federal engineers had cut off the water supply in an attempt to drain the ditch, but three to five feet of freezing water remained in the bottom. As well, the sides were stone and wooden boards. All of this made crossing it impractical, except at three bridges: One at William Street; another at Hanover Street; and one at Prussia Street (now Lafayette Boulevard.)

The Confederate skirmishers—troops posted out ahead of the main line to detect enemy assaults—used the millrace as their forward position. When the Federals broke from the western edge of the city, the rebel skirmishers opened with rifled-muskets and artillery, forcing the blue-clad infantry to attempt to deploy into attacking formations under fire. When the Federals reached the bridge on Hanover Street, they found the Confederates had retreated, but had torn up the bridge behind them.

How to Get There

From the Visitor Center, take Charlotte Street west (uphill) one block to Princess Anne Street and turn left. Follow Princess Anne two blocks to Lafayette Boulevard and turn right. Get in the right hand lane. Follow Lafayette for one block and turn right on Kenmore Avenue. (This is the site of the first crossing of the millrace. You may park along Kenmore Avenue and walk back to this site or continue along Kenmore to the second crossing site.) You are traveling along the millrace which was covered by Kenmore Avenue construction which began in 1929. Five blocks will take you to Hanover Street, site of the second bridge across the millrace. Park along the street.

Tips on Investigating

Union soldiers had to "bottleneck" to cross the millrace at Lafayette Boulevard, Hanover Street, and William Street. They took additional casualties because they were bunched up and moving slowly while crossing on the stringers. Confederate artillery on Marye's Heights had the range and began firing into the packed ranks with deadly effect. Men were mowed down by the dozens. Our imaginations would like us to envision a well-dressed, sparkling clean soldier falling to the ground as if in slow motion, death wound invisible, wrapped in the folds of his country's flag. In reality, artillery blasts tear men apart, and pieces—arms, feet, legs, hands, heads—can be seen cart-wheeling through the air above the bursts. Under artillery fire men are wounded by bones, teeth, and body parts blown violently from other men's bodies. Reports from soldiers who crossed the millrace at Prussia Street (Lafayette Boulevard) show that the scene was horrific enough to have produced a psychic imprint. David Lincoln, a soldier in Palmer's Brigade, had just set foot on the bridge over the millrace when an artillery shell tore off both of his legs. Some of the men of the 14th Connecticut stopped, transfixed by the gory spectacle. His life's blood slowly pumping out, he told the gawkers to "pass on boys. Don't stop to look at me." While Lincoln spoke, Captain William McLaughlin urged some men of the 130th Pennsylvania onto the bridge. Shells cut into his packed men. One sliced off the captain's head spewing brain matter across his troops.[3]

Some of the Union soldiers found temporary shelter in the millrace under what is now Kenmore Avenue. Inevitably, they would emerge and have to charge against the well-concealed enemy in the Sunken Road.

An investigation in 2006 with Investigative Medium Laine Crosby at Kenmore Avenue and Hanover Street (the second crossing site) provided some interesting insights into the workings of "sensitives" in the field. Not knowing anything about the history of the site, she "saw" everything from a girl and a woman running someplace to hide, to dead bodies lying out. "Some people died here; others got through … There's a partial army here of Confederates … There's an army heading from this way to that way (indicating towards the Sunken Road) … I see a canteen being thrown off into the air … some people running to fight, others just because they're scared." At one point, inside the fence that surrounds the football field, she got quite emotional about an apparently young soldier: "He's asking, 'Can you help me? I need water.' And he's calling for his mother. He's about to die."

There are reports from long time residents along Kenmore Avenue of a number of sightings of a young man. He has been seen on the street but also within some of the homes and apartments. As we know, a sudden, youthful, untimely death is one of the several reasons spirit entities may linger in a certain area on this plane we call Earth. Civil War soldiers were fairly youthful—most were in their early twenties; none but a few thought his time had come—it was always "the other fellow" who would die in the next battle; and very frequently, dying by artillery—being blown apart by a shell—was a sudden death.

There is the story of a young woman working in a Fredericksburg restaurant who lived in an apartment on Kenmore Avenue. After a hard evening at work and a nightcap, she would retire for the evening. Periodically, she would be awakened, being "touched inappropriately" by what could only have been a ghost in her locked bedroom. At least three of her friends have seen him and all describe him the same way: a young man with a page-boy haircut wearing a baggy white shirt, similar to the ill-fitting shirts issued in the 1860s by the army. A soldier, still young enough to cry for his mother, perhaps cheated out of his youth by a cruel bolt of iron fired from one of the artillery pieces on Marye's Heights, became, unbelievably, "the other fellow," one of many to die at the millrace that Kenmore Avenue now covers.

Some units that crossed the millrace in this vicinity would include the Irish Brigade, the Philadelphia Brigade, and a New Hampshire regiment.

Mercer Square or The Fair Grounds

Mercer Square no longer exists, but the site was approximately bordered on the north by present-day Mercer Street, on the east by Weedon Street, on the south by Lafayette Boulevard, and on the west by Willis Street. Currently Littlepage Street bisects what was once the Fair Grounds for the local agricultural society. Mercer Square, as Fair Grounds, contained within a high board fence a racetrack and several buildings, including stables which were converted to housing for Confederate soldiers in April of 1861. By December of 1862, much of the fence had disappeared, leaving a clear field of fire for Confederates defending the Sunken Road just below Marye's Heights.

Federal troops in the vicinity, during their assaults on December 13, 1862, attempted to cross the flat, open Fair Grounds and were forced by Confederate rifle fire to simply abandon their efforts and drop to the ground, using swales in the earth and the few remaining fence posts scattered about as meager cover.

As many as a dozen Union attacks crossed Mercer Square destined to reach within 150 yards of the stone wall at the Sunken Road before they were halted.

How to Get There

From the Fredericksburg Visitor Center, follow Charlotte Street west (uphill) to Princess Anne Street and turn left. Follow Princess Anne to Lafayette Boulevard and turn right. Follow Lafayette until you reach Littlepage Street on the right and park. A stroll down Littlepage Street will take you through the former Fair Grounds or Mercer Square. As you walk northward (from Lafayette Boulevard) you will be walking generally along the line crossed, from your right to your left, by the several Union attack waves. You will pass a number of landmarks of the battle, including the Stratton House and Sisson's Store site.

Tips on Investigating

Since numerous Union assaults were shot down in the area of the Fair Grounds, almost anywhere along Littlepage Street would seem ripe for an investigation. Littlepage is used frequently by traffic, but some of the cross streets such as Wolfe, Charlotte, Mercer or Kirkland are appropriate for EVP work as well as photography.

Units that crossed the Fair Grounds included troops from Pennsylvania, Ohio, Delaware, New Jersey, New York, Connecticut, Massachusetts, and New Hampshire.

The Stratton House

Photographs of the Fredericksburg Battlefield taken shortly after the carnage show the open plain east of Marye's Heights across which the Federal assaults took place: the millrace, the Fair Grounds, and one house that seems to be standing alone in the middle of the field of death. That house belonged to the Allen Stratton family. When the numerous attacks on the Sunken Road were turned back, the men attempted to find shelter from the storm of bullets and shells anywhere they could. They packed into and behind the Stratton House on the Littlepage Street side. The 5th New Jersey found the Stratton House an obstacle in their attack route, and when they tried to avoid it, bunched up on the north side (right side, as you face it) and made an excellent target for the Confederates in the Sunken Road. Many were killed and wounded in that area. Their flag was advanced some thirty paces beyond the Stratton House, but the brick house represented the farthest any organized units got in that area.

A soldier in the 5th New Hampshire saw, from a position of shelter at the front of the Stratton House, his captain, John Murray, killed and saw two color bearers shot down near him. Union General Darius Couch witnessed the house filled with men and the dead intermingled with the living on the Littlepage Street side of the house so thick that he could not find room for himself. Dead men and horses were rolled out to act as sheltering breastworks for the men around the Stratton House.[4] A Confederate noted that the corpses around the house and in the Stratton's nearby peach orchard were strewn so thick, one could walk without touching the ground, stepping from body to body.[5]

Stratton House

How to Get There

From the Fredericksburg Visitor Center, follow Charlotte Street west (uphill) to Princess Anne Street and turn left. Follow Princess Anne two blocks to Lafayette Boulevard and turn right. Follow Lafayette until you reach Littlepage Street on the right. Turn right on Littlepage Street and follow it three blocks to the intersection of Mercer Street. The Stratton House is on the northwest corner of Littlepage and Mercer Streets.

NOTE: The Stratton House is privately owned. DO NOT disturb the owners. An investigation using recorders, video and still cameras can be done on public areas without entering the property of the Stratton House.

Tips on Investigating

The entire area around the Stratton House was inundated with dead, wounded, dying, panicked soldiers. As you stand at the intersection of Littlepage and Mercer, allow your imagination to dissolve the streets and fill the area with the castoffs of the failed assaults upon the Confederate line at the Sunken Road. While Littlepage today is a busy street, Mercer is a little less so, and EVP might be a possibility. Some of the units that attempted to charge past the Stratton House included the 27th Connecticut, 5th New Hampshire, 35th Massachusetts, the famed "Irish Brigade," and Pennsylvanians from the famous "Philadelphia Brigade," who, at Gettysburg, as they defended against Pickett's Charge, would remember their own horror just six months before and mockingly shout, "Fredericksburg! Fredericksburg!" Try taking photos or video in the area, perhaps at dusk or afterwards, since the area is open to the public all night.

Wheelwright Shop Site

Wheelwright Shop Site

Another impediment to the Union assaults on the Sunken Road was a wheelwright shop (and an adjacent blacksmith shop) also owned by Allen Stratton. The wooden structures hardly gave Union soldiers any protection from Confederate bullets which passed right through the sides of the buildings.

How to Get There

From the Fredericksburg Visitor Center, follow Charlotte Street west (uphill) to Princess Anne Street and turn left. Follow Princess Anne to Lafayette Boulevard and turn right. Follow Lafayette until you reach Littlepage Street on the right. Turn right on Littlepage Street and follow it four blocks to the intersection of Hanover Street. Stratton's Wheelwright Shop site is about seventy-five yards south of the Hanover Street/Littlepage Street intersection on the west side of Littlepage.

Tips on Investigating

Stratton's Wheelwright Shop no longer stands. Littlepage Street is publicly accessible for investigations. Once again, be respectful of privately owned properties and conduct your investigation only from public areas. The 4th New York Infantry charged between the Stratton House and the blacksmith shop. Men from the 24th New Jersey used the blacksmith shop for its limited protection: one was shot in the head while inside.[6] Again, troops from the Irish Brigade and the Philadelphia Brigade also fought in the vicinity.

Sisson's Store

Sisson's Store Site

Another structure in the line of the Union assaults was a small grocery store and home belonging to the Sisson family. It may have been Mrs. Sisson, according to accounts from the 8th Ohio Infantry, who was dragged from the shelter of her basement in Sisson's Store, out into the firing line to help them draw water from her well. Later, after midnight, some observed in a "low brick house,"—probably Sisson's Store—through the open door "a woman, gaunt and hard-featured, with crazy hair and a Meg Merrilies face, still sitting by a smoking candle.... But what woman could sleep, though never so masculine and tough of fiber, alone in a house between two hostile armies—two corpses lying across her doorsteps, and within, almost at her feet, four more!"[7]

How to Get There

From the Fredericksburg Visitor Center, follow Charlotte Street west (uphill) to Princess Anne Street and turn left. Follow Princess Anne to Lafayette Boulevard and turn right. Follow Lafayette until you reach Littlepage Street on the right. Turn right on Littlepage Street and follow it four blocks to the intersection of Hanover Street. Sisson's Store was located in the "Y" of Hanover Street and Kirkland.

Tips on Investigating

Sisson's Store no longer stands. A building that resembles the "T" shape of the original rests in its place, probably over the same cellar. An investigation can be done from public areas around the building. Once again, do not trespass.

The Sunken Road

The Sunken Road

One of the most recognizable landmarks in all of American Military History is the Sunken Road and Stone Wall at Fredericksburg. Behind the wall stood the immovable Georgians of Brigadier General Thomas R. R. Cobb. Cobb, himself, would yield his life defending the Sunken Road, mortally wounded by a shell that crashed through the Stephens House and exploded within sight of Federal Hill, the home of his grandmother. When their commander was wounded several subordinates rushed to his aide, only to be wounded themselves: Captain Walter S.

Brewster took a mortal wound to the thigh; Lieutenant Colonel Robert T. Cook was shot in the head.

The Sunken Road was the main defensive line of Lieutenant General James Longstreet's Corps. The infantry line was backed up by artillery on Marye's Heights and Willis Hill just above and behind it. With Confederate artillery blasting Federal lines of infantry at long distance and their riflemen ensconced and virtually invisible, creating a wall of small arms fire, Union soldiers could approach no closer than fifty yards (some accounts say "thirty paces") before being driven back or crumpling to the ground. Firing ceased altogether at least once during the carnage. A woman—some say it was Martha Stephens from the Stephens House—emerged upon the field and began to minister to the wounded, checking on them and perhaps giving them water. The next day, Sergeant Richard Kirkland, a South Carolina soldier "of sublime compassion," overcome by the suffering of the enemy's wounded, took his life in his hands: loaded down with canteens, he walked the field of broken men, administering life-giving water.

Kirkland Monument

The Sunken Road became a battlefield landmark a second time in May of 1863. This time, the Federals were successful in their assaults during the Battle of Chancellorsville.

The National Park Service has restored much of the Sunken Road to its original wartime appearance.

How to Get There

From the Fredericksburg Visitor Center, go west (uphill) on Charlotte Street to Princess Anne. Turn left and follow Princess Anne Street to Lafayette Boulevard. Turn right and follow Lafayette to the National Park Service Visitor Center at the base of Marye's Heights. Park in the lot behind the building. (This would be a good time to visit the exhibits in the Visitor Center and learn a bit of the history of the battlefield you are investigating.) From the parking lot, follow the path up to the Sunken Road which overlooks the lot.

WARNING: The Sunken Road and the fields beyond are part of the National Park. Obey posted restrictions and leave the area at dusk. Full scale investigations are not recommended and interfering with other visitors' enjoyment of the area is prohibited.

Tips on Investigating

While the area is highly visited, especially during the summer months, most visitors are quiet, in awe of what happened on the site. A small scale investigation, including attempting EVP, is viable. Paranormal Investigator Scott Crownover, using his unique technique to photograph spirit energies in the daylight, has had success at the Sunken Road. Apparently there are some remnant entities which never quite left the area. Any results in this area would certainly add to the credence of the paranormal theory of residual energy being absorbed by certain environmental features (such as the stone wall), then "playing back" like a supernatural video under the correct conditions. Since the area is highly visited, remember to have a "spotter" with you to watch for live human beings entering the viewfield of your camera.

The Stephens House Site

The Stephens House Site

The Stephens House is no longer standing, but the site is marked by the National Park Service. The Stephens family had two female children and hired two slaves to help with the work. Martha Stephens was the colorful, pipe-smoking, 36-year-old matriarch of the family. Described variously as "an outcast," "uneducated, too free and too outspoken," records appear to substantiate claims that she indulged in several common-law marriages and ran a saloon in her home. Apparently an entrepreneur, she managed to buy one house, build another, and purchase a farm after the war. As well, her heart must have been in the right place; it was reported that a woman braved the field of battle to give water to wounded Confederate soldiers outside her dooryard. Some claim it was Martha Stephens, herself.[8]

Confederate General Joseph Kershaw spent time in the north room on the second floor of the Stephens House observing the battle. That is where Sergeant Kirkland found him and, driven to pity by the cries of the wounded Federals just beyond the Stephens House, requested that he be allowed to take water to the wounded to help alleviate their suffering.[9]

How to Get There

From the Fredericksburg Visitor Center, go west (uphill) on Charlotte Street to Princess Anne. Turn left and follow Princess Anne Street to Lafayette Boulevard. Turn right and follow Lafayette to the National Park Service Visitor Center. Park in the lot behind the building. From the parking lot, follow the path up to the Sunken Road which overlooks the parking lot. The Stephens House Site is a few hundred yards north of the entrance to the Sunken Road and is clearly marked.

Tips on Investigating

Martha Stephens was apparently a strong-willed, feisty woman. It would be interesting to attempt to contact her via EVP. South Carolinians, including Sergeant Richard Kirkland, General Joseph Kershaw, as well as numerous Georgians, including General T. R. R. Cobb may have left a lasting psychic impression upon the area.

The Innis House

Despite the incredible carnage and flying metal all about the Innis House during the two battles of Fredericksburg, the simple wooden structure has survived nearly 150 years and serves as a fine example of the simple life in Fredericksburg disrupted by war. It was used for a time as a sharpshooters' roost by the Confederates. Peering inside, you will still see bullet holes and damage preserved by the National Park Service, from the battles around Fredericksburg .

According to records, John and Ellen Innis (sometimes spelled "Ennis") lived there at the time of the battle. John Innis was the son of Martha Stephens, who apparently owned the land upon which the Innis House was built.

The Innis House

How to Get There

From the Fredericksburg Visitor Center, go west (uphill) on Charlotte Street to Princess Anne. Turn left and follow Princess Anne Street to Lafayette Boulevard. Turn right and follow Lafayette to the National Park Service Visitor Center. Park in the lot behind the building. From the parking lot, follow the path up to the Sunken Road which overlooks the parking lot. The Innis House is a few yards north of the Stephens House Site on the Sunken Road and is clearly marked.

Tips on Investigating

Considering the action in and around the Innis House during the battles in December 1862 and May 1863, the area should be a hot spot for paranormal activity. The house and foundation are original. If there is anything to the paranormal theory of residual energy being absorbed by the environment, then played back under certain conditions, this site would be a perfect example. Picking your time to investigate near dusk may help. Once again, obey the National Park Service regulations.

Keep in mind that, from Kirkland Avenue, near the Sisson's Store site, you are only a few dozen yards from the stone wall and the Innis House. Being a public area, you may continue your investigation after dark, once again, respecting the rights of individual private citizens who live in the area.

Maxcy Gregg Wounding Site

During the fighting on the south end of the battlefield, Meade's Union troops broke through a gap in the Confederate line. Men from the 1st and 6th Pennsylvania Reserves advanced through a wooded area toward the brigade of South Carolinians commanded by Maxcy Gregg. Because of a breakdown in communications, no skirmishers remained in Gregg's front, so his men stacked arms and lounged in reserve in the woods. Suddenly rifles cracked; Gregg's men had seen the lead elements of the Pennsylvanians coming through the woods. Gregg, unconvinced that what they saw was the enemy, rode along his line imploring his men to cease firing on their comrades. The men relaxed, re-stacked arms, and waited, unknowingly, for disaster.

The Pennsylvanians attacked. Aided by the thick underbrush and Gregg's mistake, they were upon the South Carolinians in an instant. Some of Gregg's men began firing again, and again Gregg rode to them and admonished them for firing into their own men. The Pennsylvanians loosed a volley from the woods and Gregg tumbled from his horse, a bullet slicing his spine. After a brief attempt to rally, the South Carolinians were routed and the Pennsylvanians poured into the vacuum.

Maxcy Gregg Wounding Site

The Federals drove 300 yards through the woods until their momentum died. Without realizing it, they had captured one of the main arteries—The Military Road—which would allow them to cut Lee's ability to communicate with the two wings of his army. The Yankees, at this point in the battle, had victory within their grasp.

But reinforcements were nowhere to be seen. General Franklin, in charge of the left wing of the Federal Army, had misinterpreted Burnside's orders and launched a "reconnaissance-in-force" rather than a fully supported assault. "Stonewall" Jackson's men rallied, and he ordered a massive counter-attack which drove Meade's troops back to their starting point across the railroad. After having accomplished their mission, the Pennsylvanians had to give up everything they gained because of superior officers' inability to issue or interpret orders correctly.[10]

How to Get There

From the Fredericksburg Visitor Center, follow Charlotte Street west (uphill) to Princess Anne. Turn left and follow Princess Anne Street to Lafayette Boulevard and turn right. Follow Lafayette past the National Park Service Visitor Center and across State Route 3 at the light. Get into the left lane and turn left to enter the Fredericksburg Battlefield. Follow Lee Drive. (This might be a good time to stop at several of the historic sites located on the southern end of the Fredericksburg battlefield.) After 2.5 miles, cross Lansdowne Road. Travel another 1.5 miles to Stop #5 and park.

Tips on Investigating

The Union breakthrough in this area was one of the more emotion-packed events in the battle. The Union had split the Confederate Army in half, cut the Military Road, and were close to driving a wedge between the Southern army and their capital, Richmond. Maxcy Gregg's wounding was a small, but significant occurrence in the major event of the battle. Major General George G. Meade's division was made up mostly of Pennsylvanians, including the 1st and 6th Pennsylvania Reserve regiments. Gregg's troops were from South Carolina and were scattered ignominiously by the Pennsylvanians' attack. The area is, for the most part, quiet and ideal for attempting to gather EVP. You may want to chide the South Carolinians for their actions on the field. Maxcy Gregg was deaf in life; did death restore him? Here's the time to find out!

MASS BURIAL SITES

After the battle in December 1862, individual and mass graves filled the city, from two soldiers buried outside the Baptist Church on Amelia and Princess Anne Streets,[11] to 1,363 buried in the local Fredericksburg Fair Grounds. Virtually every soldier who was killed in the Battle of Fredericksburg was buried twice. The first burials were near the spot where the killing took place. Later the bodies were exhumed and gathered together to be buried atop Marye's Heights in the National Cemetery established there in 1866. Exhumations and burials by the "Burial Corps" went on from the summer of 1866 until the fall of 1868. Eventually they interred some 15,000 soldiers from the Battle of Fredericksburg and the other major battles which took place in the area from 1863 and 1864. Of those, 12,600 are unknown, having given not only their lives for the country, but their very identities. Those soldiers whose names are known received their own plot; unknown soldiers were buried with as many as a dozen skeletons in one grave. All those buried in the National Cemetery are Union soldiers.[12]

Confederate soldiers, of course, were the late "enemy" and were disallowed from burial in the new "National" Cemetery. In spite of numerous Reconstruction regulations, former Confederates in Fredericksburg, particularly the women, banded together to form the "Ladies Memorial Association" in order to procure funds and purchase land in which to bury their soldiers. In 1867, land adjacent to the Fredericksburg Cemetery was bought and eventually some 2,000 Confederates were brought from the battlefields and interred there. Most of their identities are unknown.

WARNING: The National Cemetery and the Confederate Cemetery are NOT appropriate places in which to conduct a paranormal investigation. Supremely courageous men sacrificed their fortunes, lives, futures, and, in many cases, their identities, so that we may be able to live in the great nation in which we reside. These cemeteries are their final resting places. Decorum and good taste suggest that you pursue the hobby of paranormal investigating at the many other sites available.

There are *former* burial sites in Fredericksburg, however, that are accessible to the public.

The carnage after the battle of December was almost beyond belief. Seasoned survivors who thought they had seen the horrible harvest of combat were appalled: a southerner tallied 484 bodies in an acre; another saw a square field six hundred yards on a side were one could not walk without placing his foot upon a body. As well as whole bodies, there were bits and pieces—arms, feet, hands, legs, heads and torsos—to be gathered up and somehow "chunked" together to form enough of a body to be buried.

Under a flag of truce, Union soldiers from the 53rd Pennsylvania crossed the Rappahannock River early on December 17 to begin the onerous task of burying the bodies. They dug long trenches in the near-frozen earth, pried some of the bodies loose from the frozen sod with pick-axes, used battle-shattered boards to carry the dead heroes, and rolled them into the earth. By the end of the day some 620 bodies had been interred in the fields below Marye's Heights, most in shallow, frozen trenches. Four hundred bodies remained, however, and so the burial parties returned the next day to finish the hideous task. The Confederates were appalled at the Union soldiers' treatment of their fallen comrades; even General Lee lodged a protest. But the frozen condition of the earth made the task almost impossible.

Burial Trenches at Marye's Heights

The sites of three burial trenches have been identified by Noel G. Harrison in his excellent, two volume work, *Fredericksburg Civil War Sites.*

Long trenches for the dead were dug below Marye's Heights. The first and second were excavated in December 1862 by the Union crews that crossed the Rappahannock on December 17 and 18, 1862, for the dead from the first Battle of Fredericksburg. Another was dug in May 1864 for the men killed during the Battle of Harris' Farm. What Harrison identifies as the "westernmost north" burial trench was sixty yards long and six feet wide—just about the height of a man. The dead could be piled three deep. One hundred and thirty bodies were thus stacked in uneasy sepulture.

How to Get There

From the Fredericksburg Visitor Center, follow Charlotte Street west (uphill) seven blocks to Littlepage Street and turn right. Just before the light, turn left onto Kirkland Street. Park at about where Freeman Street intersects Kirkland. In the distance in front of you is the stone wall that bordered the Sunken Road. The "westernmost north" burial trench was about where you are now and ran approximately parallel to Freeman Street.

Tips on Investigating

This area of Fredericksburg is rather quiet and so would lend itself to attempting to gather EVP. A large number of the soldiers who fought and died in this vicinity were from Pennsylvania.[13] Addressing soldiers by their regimental numbers sometimes will garner results. "Men of the 155th Pennsylvania, are you still here?" or "Soldiers of the 69th Pennsylvania, I know you fought well here. Would anyone like to talk with us?" Remember to give them plenty of time to answer—six or seven long, slow breaths.

This area is also open at night. Photographs or video made with "night-shot" or "near infrared" cameras may yield results. If you have outfitted your camera according to Scott Crownover's daylight spirit photography technique, however, you can attempt to take photos of spirit entities anytime.

Another burial trench was dug farther to the east and was probably the first dug, since it was originally created by Union troops under fire for protection. It contained 609 bodies—the approximate number claimed to have been buried on December 17 before the burial details re-crossed the river for the night. This trench was about the length of a football field and, again, about six feet wide. It ran south from the Telegraph Road—now Hanover Street—and paralleled the stone wall approximately 250 yards to the east.

How to Get There

From the Fredericksburg Visitor Center, follow Charlotte Street west (uphill) seven blocks to Littlepage Street and turn right. Park on Littlepage Street near the light. Walk to Hanover Street and turn right. The "easternmost north" (as Harrison describes it) burial trenches extended south from Hanover Street, roughly paralleling Littlepage Street. From Hanover Street you can attempt an investigation.

Tips on Investigating

Hanover Street is one of the busier thoroughfares in Fredericksburg, so EVP may be out of the question. Photos and video, however, may be attempted. Again, across this area charged the Pennsylvanians. Invoking the spirits from the Keystone State may provide results.

Finally, what Harrison identifies as the "south" burial trench, was excavated around May 19 and 20, 1864, to hold the bodies of the soldiers who were killed during one of the final stages of the Battle of Spotsylvania known as the Battle of Harris Farm. This trench was some 200 yards long and six feet wide. Harrison estimates the number of burials were less than 500 bodies. The trench ran north from Lafayette Boulevard about 100 yards to the east of the Sunken Road along, or just to the east, of what is now Willis Street.

How to Get There

From the Fredericksburg Visitor Center, travel west (uphill) on Charlotte Street one block to Princess Anne Street. Turn left on Princess Anne and follow it to Lafayette Boulevard. Turn right on Lafayette. Follow Lafayette to Willis Street on the right. Turn right on Willis and park.

Tips on Investigating

The Battle of Harris Farm began as a reconnaissance in force by Confederate General Richard Ewell's Corps along the Courthouse Road from Spotsylvania to Fredericksburg. Instead of finding that Grant had withdrawn, as Lee mistakenly suspected, Ewell ran into some relatively green troops—Heavy Artillery regiments, pulled from the defenses around Washington and pressed into service as infantrymen. They fought stubbornly as a division commanded by Brigadier General Robert O. Tyler. Units that distinguished themselves—and paid a fearful price in lives—were the 1st Massachusetts Heavy Artillery and the 1st Maine Heavy Artillery. The "Heavies" lost over 1,500 men, a number of whom would end up buried in the "south" burial trench, along Willis Street.

Willis Street is very near the Sunken Road and parts of it are quiet enough to attempt EVP, possibly using the regimental names of the 1st Maine and 1st Massachusetts Heavy Artillery. The Willis Street area is open to the public after dark. You may want to attempt photography or videography from the public sidewalk areas.

There are no known bodies still buried in the trenches. They were exhumed between 1866 and 1868 and re-buried in the National Cemetery on Marye's Heights.

WARNING: National Park Service areas, including the Sunken Road and parking areas, are closed after sunset. DO NOT attempt an investigation in these areas after dark. The burial trenches are now under private homes or yards. Attempt

an investigation only from public property, such as the street or sidewalk. DO NOT disturb private citizens in their homes.

Corporation Burying Ground (Hurkamp Park)

Hurkamp Park

While the land for Fredericksburg's cemetery had been set aside for nearly thirty years, the first burial wasn't until 1803. By the 1850s, however, there was no more room within the brick walls of the cemetery and it was closed to burials. It was named "The Corporation Burying Ground," after the fact that the City of Fredericksburg was a "corporation." During the Second Battle of Fredericksburg in May 1863, Union troops camped in the Corporation Burying Ground.

By 1881, all the tombstones were removed. Many of the bodies, however, were not. It is not uncommon, when cemeteries are abandoned and the land is about to be re-used, for an attempt to be made to exhume all the earthly remains of the dead. The efforts are hardly ever 100 percent successful. Still, the area was renamed "Hurkamp Park," and is presently open to the public.

How to Get There

Hurkamp Park is located between George and William Streets on Prince Edward Street. From the Fredericksburg Visitor Center, exit onto Caroline Street. Drive two blocks to George Street and turn left. Follow George Street three blocks to Prince Edward Street. Cross Prince Edward Street and Hurkamp Park will be on your right.

Tips for Investigating

While decorum and good taste dictate that you should not do a paranormal investigation in a National Cemetery, since the Corporation Burying Ground has been abandoned (at least by living mourners and *most* of the dead) it might be fertile ground for an investigation. Some areas of the Park are far enough away from the streets to provide a good, quiet venue for attempting to get EVP. Try asking, "What is your last name?" or "Who is president?" and see what kind of response you receive.

Potter's Field

Potter's Field with Maury Condominiums in Background

As recently as February, 2007, human remains were unearthed at a construction site where a developer is transforming a former school into luxury condominiums. The remains are believed to have come from an African-American cemetery once located where Maury School was built in 1919. The cemetery apparently expanded into what is now the William Street parking lot for the Fredericksburg newspaper, *The Free Lance-Star*. It was thought that all the bodies were removed to Shiloh Cemetery on Littlepage Street, but, as invariably happens, not all the bodies were located. The remains were found between the wall of the school's gymnasium and Day Street, a gravel road that runs along the edge of the parking lot. The cemetery dated back to the mid-1800s. The cemetery was either very large, or some of the bodies were not buried alongside others. Ruth Coder Fitzgerald, a Fredericksburg Historian wrote in 1999 that, even after the school was built, bodies remained buried on the school grounds. Before the football field was built for budding young athletes, Fitzgerald wrote that "every time it rained, bones came out of the ground."[14]

How to Get There

From the Fredericksburg Visitor Center follow Charlotte Street west (uphill) to Princess Anne and turn left. Follow Princess Anne to Lafayette Boulevard and turn right. Follow Lafayette to Kenmore Avenue and turn right. Follow Kenmore to Hanover Street and park on Kenmore. The gates to Maury Field are located on the Hanover Street side of the field and may be open during the day. Maury School Condominium Complex can be seen above the field.

Tips on Investigating

Tree in Potter's Field

Investigative Medium Laine Crosby visited Maury Field in 2006 and felt strong emotions at the Kenmore Avenue side of the field. There is a large, old tree at the Kenmore Avenue/Hanover Street corner of the fenced-in field. At the tree she "saw,' (psychically, of course), the very strong energy of a man in his early 20s, with long, dark hair. She said he was about ten feet to the Kenmore Avenue side of the tree, that he wore a blue jacket and gray trousers. But there was something wrong with the trousers. The right, leg, she saw, was destroyed from the knee down, probably by an artillery shell. Laine felt the area near the tree would be ripe for obtaining EVP. She called the area of the field along the Kenmore Avenue fence, "The Dying Field" and saw scores of wounded and dead men lined up, with their heads towards Kenmore Avenue and their feet towards the school. In a second interview with her in August 2007, she mentioned, remarkably, that there could have been burials in the field, but she felt that they were moved.

St. George's Episcopal Church

St. George's Episcopal Church

St. George's Episcopal Church boasts the oldest continuing congregation in Fredericksburg. Its inception dates to 1732. It was George Washington's church when he lived at Ferry Farm. The present St. George Episcopal Church was built in 1849 upon the site of the original. This building is actually the third church to be built on the site. The main sanctuary has hardly changed from the original, and so the Civil War era worshippers would still recognize it—if they had the power to return, which some reports indicate they may very well have! The side balconies were added after the Civil War. The church remained in service for both Union and Confederate soldiers, depending upon which occupied the town during the war.

The church was damaged in the Union bombardment in December 1862. Confederates used the church during the great Christian revival in the Confederate Army in 1863. It was used as a hospital for the casualties from the Battle of the Wilderness in 1864.

The pews were permanently installed rendering them unremovable by hospital orderlies or Union soldiers. Some pews in town were cut up and used as headboards for gravesites, but the seating in St. George's is the same used during the war.

There are three Tiffany stained-glass windows in the church.

Beside the church is a cemetery in which the oldest gravestone dates back to 1752. Buried here are Colonel John Dandridge, father of Martha Washington, and William Paul, John Paul Jones's brother.

During the Battle of Fredericksburg in December 1862, the church was used by the Union Army as a hospital. One wounded northerner described what he saw outside the building along the stairs: "dead soldiers piled on either side as high as the top step, and the fence hanging full of belts, cartridge boxes, canteens, and haversacks."[15] The fence and the steps are the originals.

But it is what has been seen inside the church, dating back to 1858, that interests ghost hunters.

The original 1858 story, involving a young woman watching a worshipper vanish before her eyes is found in the 1930 publication, *Virginia Ghosts,* by Marguerite DuPont Lee. It is an example of an intelligent, or interactive haunting and was related in an earlier section of this book.

In addition to the 1858 story, according to the local police, the K-9 police dogs are particularly nervous inside and outside of the church. The dogs especially react at the door to the balcony.[16] "There aren't too many police officers who haven't had an experience in St. George's," according to one. The police will check the doors at night to make sure they are locked—and they are. An hour or so later, they will check again and they will be unlocked. Officers will hear footsteps walking through the sanctuary when there is no one visible; they will hear the benches creaking as if someone just sat down in them. The caretaker was working in the cemetery and felt someone come up behind him and touch him on the shoulder, but when he turned around to see what the person wanted, no one was there.

How to Get There

From the Fredericksburg Visitor Center travel 2 blocks on Caroline Street and turn left on George Street. St. George's is on the corner of George and Princess Anne Streets.

Tips on Investigating

The doors to St. George's Episcopal Church are open to the public until 9:00 P.M. A preliminary afternoon investigation inside the church with an investigative medium brought some mixed results. Numerous photos showed nothing out of the ordinary—one faint "orb" appeared. The medium, however, mentioned that the church pews were full of parishioners from all eras—from Colonial to the 21st Century—showing how remarkable some "sensitives" can be.

The cemetery next to the church, however, may be a little more active. Photos taken after dark have produced orbs, wisps of paranormal mist, and strange colors.

It is recommended that you confine your investigation to the exterior of the building. Certainly there must be some activity near the front door where the bodies of Union soldiers were piled to the top of the steps.

Willis Cemetery, Willis Hill

The Willis Cemetery received its first burials in 1756, long before even the thought of fratricidal strife shadowed the land, before there even was a United States to tear asunder. A hundred years before the War Between the States turned Willis Hill and Marye's Heights into a synonym for slaughter, the site was the gentile home and final resting place for members of the Willis, Welford, and Carter families. During the battle in December 1862, the ambulance corps used the sturdy brick walls as shelter as did the 15th South Carolina placed there in support of the famed Washington Artillery. Damage caused by Union artillery fire can still be seen in the posts at the entrance to the cemetery.[17]

How to Get There

From the Fredericksburg Visitor Center, go west (uphill) on Charlotte Street to Princess Anne. Turn left and go to Lafayette. Turn right and follow Lafayette to the National Cemetery. Park in the National Park Service Visitor Center lot and climb Marye's Heights to the National Cemetery. To the north (your right) at the summit you will see a brick wall. Enter the brick wall and follow the path to the left to the Willis Cemetery.

Willis Cemetery

Tips on Investigating

In attempting EVP on Willis Hill, the men of the 15th South Carolina, or the Washington Artillery can be addressed. Colonel J. B. Walton was the commander of the Washington Artillery of New Orleans.

The Baptist Church

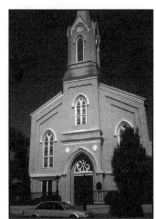

The Baptist Church sheltered wounded as a makeshift hospital in 1862, 1863, and 1864. During the December 1862 battle, at least two Confederate shells struck the church and one exploded within. At least one more solid shot passed into the church. William Child, a Union surgeon noted that the church floor was "covered with Union wounded." Attempting to continue operating after dark, surgeons lighted candles which drew artillery fire and soon had to be extinguished.

In May 1863, the church basement was utilized and covered with dead and wounded men. Again in May 1864, the church opened its doors for the wounded: the baptismal pool was used to bathe the

Baptist Church

wounded and operations were done in the study of the pastor behind the pulpit.

Between 1866 and 1868, two bodies were exhumed from outside the church and taken to the National Cemetery.

How to Get There

From the Fredericksburg Visitor Center take Caroline Street north four blocks to Amelia and turn left. The Baptist Church is in the next block at the corner of Amelia and Princess Anne.

Tips on Investigating

While you may be able to visit within the church during the hours it is open, it is best to conduct any investigation outside the building, perhaps on the sidewalk, which is open to the public.

The Planter's Hotel

Planter's Hotel

Construction on the Planter's Hotel was completed by 1843. If high amounts of human energy is one of the reasons for residual hauntings, then surely the Planter's Hotel must rank as one of the sites that shows the most promise for an investigation. Prior to the Civil War, the corner of William and Charles Streets where the Planter's Hotel building stands was the site of a number of slave auctions. In fact, the stone "auction block," still stands at the corner. One can only imagine the horror of an African American slave standing upon the block, knowing that the next bid could send him or her far from home and family.

In May 1864, the Planter's Hotel became a hospital for Michigan troops of the Federal 9th Corps.

How to Get There

From the Fredericksburg Visitor Center, follow Caroline Street north two blocks to George Street and turn left. Follow George two blocks to Charles Street and turn right. Follow Charles one block to William and park. The building that once was the Planter's Hotel is on the north west corner of William and Charles.

Tips on Investigating

The old Planter's Hotel Building is private residences and so an investigation inside is out of the question. Enough happened outside, however, to create residual energy. Records indicate that slaves of Mrs. H. H. Coalter of Chatham were sold off the block around the end of December 1857. Originally, Mrs. Coalter had set them free in her will. You can imagine their agony when the Virginia Supreme Court of Appeals declared her wish invalid, and the slaves were sold at auction.

In addition, when the hotel was used as a hospital, in May 1864, a nurse left an account, naming some of the soldiers and describing their horrific wounds. A Captain Donohue of the 8th Michigan and Lieutenant Joss of the 2nd Michigan both had high leg amputations and were not expected to live. Several men were shot in the face, including a Sergeant Clark, whose tongue was so swollen he could not talk and could only ingest liquids. Apparently, there were hundreds of similar cases in and around the hotel.[18]

Chatham

Chatham

Chatham is one of the more documented and historic buildings in all of Fredericksburg. It is also the home of one of Fredericksburg's most famous ghosts, the Lady in White. Across the Rappahannock River from Fredericksburg on the bluff sits "Chatham," built between 1768 and 1771 by William Fitzhugh. George Washington spent many happy hours there. It claims to be the only house in America visited by both Washington and Abraham Lincoln. According to historians, young Robert E. Lee courted his wife-to-be, Miss Mary Custis, in the lovely rose garden. During the Battle of Fredericksburg in December 1862, it was known as the Lacy House, after its owner, and was used as a headquarters for the Union Army. It was also used as a hospital during the Battle of Fredericksburg in December 1862, and Clara Barton, founder of the Red Cross, and the American poet, Walt Whitman, nursed wounded soldiers there. It is now owned by the National Park Service and serves as headquarters for the Fredericksburg and Spotsylvania National Military Park.

There are periodic sightings, like clockwork, of the famous White Lady of Chatham. The wife of a former owner in the early 20th Century saw her on several occasions in the famous garden of Chatham, strolling casually along the path leading to the terrace below, then vanishing as suddenly as she had appeared. She is the classic "residual" haunting. Her story is as mysterious as it is sad.

The story comes down to us through Marguerite DuPont Lee in her 1930s book *Virginia Ghosts*. She tells of Mrs. Randolph Howard, who confided to only a few friends that she had seen a strange woman in white, pacing up and down the garden path which led by marble steps to the terrace below. It was sometime in the afternoon, June 21. She had kept the sighting a secret; she didn't want to frighten her servants. Some time later she was entertaining a friend who happened to be a scholar of French literature. He began to tell her of an interesting discovery he had made while poring over some books written in French in a library in Newark, New Jersey. He was leafing through a collection of ghost stories when the names "Washington" and "Chatham" leapt from the pages. He began to tell Mrs. Howard the story.

It appears that a young Englishwoman of a noble family fell in love with a common "dry-salter," or preserver of food. They made plans for an elopement, which were soon discovered by her father. He immediately took his daughter to America where they met the Fitzhughs and stayed for a while at Chatham. Unbeknownst to the father, the dry-salter followed, contacted the young lady, and they planned their elopement once again. Again the father discovered the plan and locked her in her room every night. The dry-salter planned her escape via rope ladder from her room to his boat moored on the river below. At the appointed hour, she descended the ladder and dropped into the arms of none-other than George Washington, himself. The plot had been discovered by an aide to Washington who had the dry-salter locked up. Washington took the girl to her father who returned with her back to England. There, he married her off quickly. In spite of bearing her husband ten children, she apparently continued to dream of her first love and their planned elopement from Chatham. On June 21, 1790, on her death bed, she predicted that she would return to Chatham from the Other World to walk the terrace, her favorite spot, as a spirit.

She apparently does return. It was she whom Mrs. Howard saw that afternoon, strolling through the terrace garden. She returns punctually, every seven years on June 21, the anniversary of her death, and walks sometime between noon and midnight.

How to Get There

From the Fredericksburg Visitor center, take Charlotte Street east (downhill) to Sophia and turn left. Follow Sophia three blocks and turn right at the light on William Street. As you cross the Rappahannock River, get in the left-hand lane. Turn left on Chatham Heights Road, then left on Chatham Lane. (Brown and white National Park Service signs will help guide you.)

Tips on Investigating

The fabled White Lady of Chatham was supposed to appear in 2007. Although the National Park Service graciously kept Chatham open to the public until midnight on June 21, 2007, no reports of the White Lady have surfaced as of this writing. Investigative Medium Laine Crosby was supposed to accompany me and my wife Carol on our June 21, 2007, "stake out" of the mansion and grounds, but a series of bizarre circumstances prevented her from coming. Instead, she "remote viewed" Chatham and gave us some remarkable information over our cell phones from her home outside of Virginia.[19]

First, she began describing the grounds and the building of Chatham. Her description of a balconied façade did not match what we saw before us—until we saw a photo, taken at the time of the Civil War which showed the elegant balcony on the front (river side) of the building. I was having trouble getting EVP; the machine recorded nothing but my voice. Without ever having been to Chatham, Laine asked, "Do you see those two trees near the building?" I looked up to see two ancient catalpa trees, witnesses to much of the storied history of Chatham. "Go over and stand between them. Try getting EVP." Sure enough, standing between the "witness" trees, I began gathering the gruff roars and frustrated grumblings of those who were trying to speak for the first time in a dozen or more decades.

The trees stand outside the windows to the room where the surgeons plied their trade on wounded, sometimes unwilling, patients. Extremities were unceremoniously sliced, then sawn off and tossed roughly out the windows to form hideous piles below the sills. Arms and hands and legs and feet, once precious, lifelong possessions of the young men who fought in the battles around Fredericksburg, were treated like so many logs, carted off and burned to get rid of them. No doubt the agony—physical, mental, emotional—which swirled through the area between the house and the trees, was like a psychic tornado, impressing everything around it, and leaving its stamp on the earth, the building, and the trees themselves. Laine felt it fifty miles away and a hundred and forty-odd years after the fact.

Fredericksburg's history is broad and deep, reaching all the way back to 1608 when John Smith explored up the Rappahannock to the Falls. It is no wonder then, that Fredericksburg ghosts have appeared from virtually every era in its history, to people in virtually every succeeding era in its history.

The Chimneys

"The Chimneys" was built around 1770 by an immigrant Scotsman John Glassel who was a merchant. Loyal to the crown, when the Revolution broke out, he left his property to his brother and returned to Scotland. The property has changed hands and has assumed many incarnations since then.

Apparently, one of the early occupants, probably a young woman, played the harp in the parlor, for it is from that area that the sweet strains of a phantom harp are heard upon occasion, playing a melody many decades off the list of popular songs. Sometimes the refrain is accompanied by a ghostly singer.

The Chimneys

Years after the harp and its player were gone, some occupants of the house bought a piano. One evening a young woman sat down and began to accompany herself on the piano. She heard the front door (which is the one towards the Rappahannock River) open and close. She was surprised to hear footsteps approach. She knew there were guests out front and called out a request for the person trying to frighten her to identify himself. The only answer was the plodding footsteps which, by now, had reached the doorway. She turned apprehensively toward the sound, but as the phantom footfalls approached the piano, she could see no one. Her piano recital suddenly came to an end when someone, quite invisible, sat down on the piano bench next to her and placed an unseen, icy hand upon her shoulder.

One particular night when "The Chimneys" was still a residence, a woman was awakened by a chill in the air. The chill grew perceptibly colder as she approached her youngest son's bedroom. She took a blanket from a closet and entered his room. To her astonishment, there was another male child asleep in the bed next to her son. She could not identify him because his face was half-covered with the sheet, but she assumed that perhaps her sleeping husband had invited one of the neighbor-boys to spend the night. She covered the two, and went back to bed herself. The next morning when her husband awakened she asked who the boy was he had invited to spend the night with their son. She was met with an incredulous look and the affirmation that he had not invited anyone to spend the night. At that moment, her son came down for breakfast and confirmed that indeed, he slept alone that night. And while the woman's original mission was to cover her son to ward off the cold, the night—at least in the rest of the house—had been overly warm. A quick examination of her son's bed revealed to the woman that only one child had spent the night there.

Ghosts at "The Chimneys" are nothing new. Dr. Brodie Herndon who owned the house in the mid-19th Century claimed that the house was haunted. Some of the paranormal events he recorded continue to this day, such as, doorknobs being turned by invisible hands and doors opening by themselves. Apparently in Mr. Brodie's time a woman saw her uncle standing in one of the rooms across the hall. By the time she entered the room, it was empty. This apparition was what is known as a "harbinger," for her uncle died three days later.

And auditory apparitions, the most common, also occur: The sound of china crashing to the floor; upon inspection of the room, nothing is amiss. Heavy footsteps are heard in the hall when no one is there; doors are heard slamming, and occasionally, someone will watch as a rocking chair starts moving back and forth—with no one seated in it.

Second Floor of The Chimneys

Some of the more recent happenings involve child ghosts. The apparition of a little boy is seen roaming about upstairs. There is the rumor of a little boy who fell from the balcony to his death many years ago. He also apparently doesn't like a certain door upstairs to be closed because, as often as they close it and leave at night, the next morning the door is open. A little girl also walks the floor upstairs then is seen to vanish, as well as the apparition of a grown woman. The owners of the restaurant housed in The Chimneys spent their first night in Fredericksburg in an upstairs room. They had cats—animals are often more sensitive to the paranormal than humans—and the cats did not sleep all night. As well, the two woke the next morning to find that each had dreamed all night long of children.

The stories about the famous "Underground Railroad," that clandestine matrix of people, routes, and safe-houses for runaway slaves in Antebellum America, are as mysterious as they are romantic. Most of what we know about the system of transferring slaves from slave-holding states to freedom comes from *after* the Civil War, since harboring escaped slaves, throughout most of American history, was a crime, and those involved were reluctant to speak about it. In spite of that, the Virginia Abolition Society was formed in the 1780s.

But legislators representing slaveholders fought back. In the Fugitive Slave Act of 1793, rights to slaves as property became constitutional. Because of the Fugitive Slave Act of 1850, it became a violation of Federal law to assist escaping slaves, and slaves were forced to be returned to their masters, inflicting heavy fines and jail terms upon those aiding slaves' escape. Regardless, by 1830 the Underground Railroad was in full operation in the North and the South.

Railroad terminology was used to throw off slave-catchers: Safe houses were called "depots" or "stations," and were located one nights' walk apart; guides to escaping slaves were called "conductors"; "agents" offered their homes as day-shelters for escapees; "superintendents" controlled the operations in an entire state. During the day, slaves were hidden in barns, beneath floor-boards, in false rooms, the cog-pits of mills, and damp cellars. They often waited days for forged "documents of passage" to arrive. Night escapes were on foot, in false bottoms in wagons, on the top of railroad cars, by canoe, schooner, or steamer. The Chesapeake Bay was sought because of its access into the North, so the waterways draining into the Bay—such as the Rappahannock—were desired routes. Indeed, several maps of the routes of the escapees on the Underground Railroad show Fredericksburg in the center.

At this writing, there is no documented evidence that The Chimneys was ever used as a depot on the Underground Railroad. There is, however, evidence from the Other World that someone, desperate to escape, remained in the cellar of the building far too long. This is a story of two kinds of escape: one from slavery, the other from death.

On the evening of April 21, 2006, a medium—a psychic—whom I work with during paranormal investigations, explored The Chimneys along with several others interested in the paranormal history of the building. After getting her impressions of several of the rooms, including the strong presence of a seafarer, she descended into the cellar.

The cellar of The Chimneys is currently used as a storage area for the businesses in the building. The Medium approached the main area of the cellar and commented, "I feel like I can't leave, but I'm not a prisoner, and I'm not locked in."

"Channeling" is a psychic phenomenon wherein the Medium becomes a conduit for the deceased, feeling, moving, and speaking as if they were the dead person.

The Medium was later asked if she was channeling someone dead from the past. Her response was that she was merely repeating, verbatim, what she was hearing in the cellar that night. According to my wife, Carol, who accompanied her into the cellar, after passing through the door into the room, the Medium received the name "Nicodemus." Her commentary went as follows:

> Don't know where I am, came with others.
>
> They got papers. They left.
>
> Can't leave without papers. Miss Hattie bring papers. Can't read, can't write, don't know what in papers. Need papers to leave.
>
> Others come, get papers, leave. Don't understand....
>
> *(Medium interjects at this point that she sensed that there was something wrong with his one hand, that his hand was crippled or injured in some way.)*
>
> I work, back strong, I carry things.
>
> *(She points to some objects piled in the corner)*
>
> I carry that ... I work, need papers, don't understand.
>
> People in house don't know I here.
>
> *(Carol asks if his name is Nicodemus)*
>
> No, just what they call me. Hattie not her name, just what they call her.
>
> Hear music, must be quiet ... dark, Miss Hattie bring papers.
>
> More came. They got papers, left, said they'd come back for me. Never came.
>
> Music stopped, quiet ... scared, can't leave
>
> *(The Medium suddenly says she thought she smelled smoke and was on the verge of tears at this point. She also had the sense that he had died there, in that cellar.)*

The Medium's olfactory impression of a fire is interesting because the records show that in 1799 a huge fire destroyed much of this neighborhood. It was rebuilt, but burned again in 1823. This may give a clue as to which approximate period she was "tapping into."

Carol called me into the cellar, and the Medium asked me to attempt to get some EVP. My technique is to ask a question pertinent to the past into a digital recorder, then pause with the recorder set on "voice activation." In complete silence, the machine began to record.

Two sessions were attempted. The first session yielded rough, staccato answers to my questions, yet hardly decipherable as words. But in answer to the question, "Nicodemus, are you trying to get your freedom?" the answer was an immediate, loud, and clearly audible, "Oh, yeah." Prior to the second session, the Medium recommended that I tell "Nicodemus" that he could go now, that he didn't need his papers, and that he didn't need to wait for Hattie, which I did. As I stood there in the darkening cellar, I felt an extremely cold spot touch my right arm and remain there for about five seconds. Then it was replaced by a hot sensation, then back to regular temperature. After the session, I mentioned this to the Medium. She, too, had felt the presence of "Nicodemus" leave the cellar.

How to Get There
The Chimneys is diagonally across Caroline Street and within walking distance from the Fredericksburg Visitor Center.

Tips on Investigating
The lower floors of The Chimneys are used for retail businesses. Noise and echoes make obtaining uncluttered EVP all but impossible, even on the upper floors. Interior photos can be taken throughout the building.

Kenmore
Kenmore was built in 1752 by Fielding Lewis. In 1775, he was contracted by the Virginia Assembly to manufacture small arms for the Revolution. When funds were not forthcoming from the government, Lewis began using his own personal fortune to fund the manufacturing throughout the war. In spite of the fact that he was the brother-in-law of George Washington, the government reneged on its bargain to pay Lewis for the arms. Fielding Lewis died in 1781, no doubt perturbed at the government he supported so faithfully that nearly cost him his home. And though he died trying to keep his beloved Kenmore from his creditors, it seems that he has found a way to return

Kenmore

For a while inhabitants of the house were hearing strange noises both at night and in broad daylight. A man's heavy footsteps have been heard on the stairs and in the halls; the noise of footsteps on gravel and the sound of boots scraping on the stone threshold. The doors as well hold strange secrets. On certain nights, doorknobs will turn, but no one will enter the room. For several days a door to one of the bedrooms could not be opened. A caretaker swore he would call a carpenter the next day to fix the problem. In the morning, the door was discovered open.

Though many people believe that ghosts manifest themselves only at night, one day a woman saw the form of Colonel Fielding Lewis himself standing in the upstairs room. He was clothed in the garb of the mid-18th Century and appeared to be reading an ancient paper which he held in his hand.

Later, another young woman was walking down the hall, and upon passing the Colonel's office, glanced in to see, seated at a table, reviewing what appeared to be business papers, the man who lost virtually all his possessions in aiding his country. It seems as if, even in death, Fielding Lewis is trying to save Kenmore.

Finally, one of the women who owned the house, recalled, on an oppressively hot summer's day, how she stood with some friends in Betty Washington Lewis's bedroom and, in spite of the sultry, still air, she felt a cold breeze waft across the back of her head. She remarked to her two companions about it and that she believed the room they were in was haunted. At that moment, their attention was drawn to the wardrobe standing in the room by a click made by the handle. Slowly, as if to affirm the woman's belief in spirits, the wardrobe door swung open untouched by human hands.

How to Get There

From the Fredericksburg Visitor Center, drive north on Caroline Street four blocks to Amelia Street and turn left. Follow Amelia six blocks until it dead-ends at the Confederate Cemetery and Washington Avenue. Turn right on Washington Avenue. Bear right at the "do not enter" signs, then bear left to continue on Washington Avenue. Kenmore is immediately on your right and parking spaces are marked.

The Kenmore Inn

A brief history of the Kenmore Inn reveals that it was built in 1793. George Washington may have spent some time here since Fielding Lewis once owned the property, and Lewis most certainly would have entertained his brother-in-law. Lewis may have lived in the building while construction of Kenmore Plantation was going on.

During the Civil War, Union soldiers used the basement as stalls for their horses. There is a garage that has been re-done into a casual dining area, but during the war it was used as a hospital. Because it was a brick building and used as a Union hospital, may explain why it wasn't ransacked and burned by the Union Army. One of the managers has found bullets and buttons in the yard, as well as a whiskey flask, and some vertebra that might be human.

The Kenmore Inn

Halloween, 2005. Two of the waitstaff and one of the managers of the inn, were standing in the front hallway under one of the two chandeliers in the main entrance. They were talking and, it being Halloween, the manager happened to mention something about "ghosts." Just at that moment, the light in the chandelier over her head "flashed." They all looked at each other incredulously, and moved out of the room. About five minutes later they were talking again, mentioning that the flashing light seemed kind of odd. The manager again mentioned the word "ghost" and the same chandelier flashed. It never flashed before and hasn't since. Of course, she admitted that she hasn't used the word "ghost" in the hallway since that Halloween.

Several inspectors have come to inspect the kitchen and public restrooms. A female inspector asked to see the men's room. The manager said, "Go ahead, there's no one here now." The inspector went downstairs and heard water running in the men's room. She came back upstairs to tell the manager but the manager said, "That's impossible, I'm the only one here. Go on inside." So the inspector opened the door, and a huge cloud of what she described as steam came pouring out. She saw that the hot water was on as far as it could go. But everyone in the Kenmore knows that the water down in the basement never gets hot enough to produce steam, and certainly not enough steam to create a man-sized cloud of mist. One must wonder if it was steam, or paranormal mist the inspector witnessed. The same inspector was reaching under the dishwashing sink to inspect the plumbing. She thought she'd put her hand in water because it felt so cold. On second thought, she said it felt like someone had put a cold hand right on top of her hand. Of course there was no water, and no one—at least no one visible—lying beneath the sink with ice-cold hands. Also, periodically, the manager will go downstairs to the kitchen and the gas burners will be turned on full blast.

Room 203, which is actually two adjoining rooms, had two different guests at two different times say that they felt like someone was stroking their hair. Another time, a woman was sleeping in the front room and her two children were in the back room in the twin beds. She woke up in the middle of the night and thought one of her children had sat down on her bed. But when she looked up she saw nothing. She went to see if one of her children had gotten up, but they were both still asleep.

In the fine dining room in one of the chandeliers two of the lights will periodically flicker. These are not the same chandeliers in the hallway that "flashed." The lights will go for months and nothing will happen, then they will flicker again.

At the end of May 2006, the manager heard something she'd never heard before in the Kenmore: disembodied voices. The first was a very deep, male voice, saying 4 or 5 words coming from near the floor by room 208. Then she heard a woman's voice coming from the stairwell in the kitchen leading to the first floor. She couldn't understand the words, but it was definitely a female.

How to Get There

From the Fredericksburg Visitor Center, follow Caroline Street six blocks to Fauquier Street and turn left. Follow Fauquier one block to Princess Anne and turn left. The Kenmore Inn is on the right, halfway down that block. Parking is on either side of the street.

Tips on Investigating

If you are visiting Fredericksburg overnight to specifically hunt for ghosts, it doesn't get any better than the Kenmore Inn: it is a fine restaurant and Bed and Breakfast. In the cellar is a quaint bar where food can also be ordered. If you rent one of the haunted rooms mentioned above, you will be able to set up night-shot video equipment overnight or attempt EVP as often as you wish.

In 2005, while staying at the Kenmore, I decided to attempt some EVP in room 203 which was vacant at the time. As I've said before, I am not very sensitive to paranormal manifestations. No sooner did I enter the first of the two rooms than I started to get chills down my back, and had the hair on my arms stand up. I asked a few questions into my recorder, but became so uncomfortable that I had to leave. Replaying the recording, I found I had gotten some very strong EVP. Chills or not, I went back into the room.

Again, the chills ran down my back and the hair on my arms stood. I literally had to force myself farther back into the second room, in spite of the intensifying feelings of cold and of not being alone. I asked more questions into the recorder, and finally had to leave. The feeling of being uncomfortable, of being an intruder, was overwhelming. Replaying the recording again yielded loud, seemingly angry roars. I thought about going back into room 203, but found myself utterly exhausted. I called it a night for my ghost hunting.

Charlotte Street

Charlotte Street is the setting for one of Fredericksburg's most famous ghosts—The Headless Blue Lady of Charlotte Street. Author L. B. Taylor recounts the story in his book *Ghosts of Fredericksburg*.

There seemed to be a spate of unexplainable occurrences centering on the 500 block of Charlotte Street in May 1974.

One harbinger to the weird sightings was the strange entrance and exit of an invisible being from one of the homes. A woman was finishing the dishes one afternoon when she distinctly heard her screen door and then the front door open. She thought it was her grandchildren coming in for a visit and called to them. No one answered. She walked into the living room to see why her grandchildren were being so uncharacteristically silent to find that no one—at least no one visible—had entered her home. She went back to her dishes when she heard the door open again, this time in reverse order: the inner door first, then the screen door—as if someone were leaving her home. She quickly went out the front door to see who it was, only to see ... no one.

Yet another omen came when the residents saw a number of Fredericksburg police cars gathered outside of the Charlotte Street home of a woman who worked for the FBI. She had some semi-classified documents in an upstairs room in her home which she always kept locked. She had gone upstairs to work, unlocked the door to the room and was stunned at what she saw. Pandemonium had struck: file cabinets were upturned and their contents strewn about the room, yet not a single document had been taken. Adding to the mystery was how anyone could have entered the locked room, or how they could have exited without leaving a window open or at least unlocked.

Still another bizarre incident caught the woman's attention that same strange week in May 1974. It was night on Charlotte Street when she looked out her back window to see what she described as an "amorphous form with a bluish cast" near the magnificent 18th Century mansion called Federal Hill. She identified it, by its form, as the figure of a woman. But instead of walking like a normal, living woman, it floated about the ground as it approached the mansion. One other odd thing stood out, to the observer's horror: the blue woman was headless!

Again, during the month that seemed to have no end in Fredericksburg, the Lady in Blue was seen on Charlotte Street just a few doors from the previous sightings.

A man was on his sunporch one night watching television. He stood to change the channels and got the uneasy feeling that he was being watched. He turned and saw the mere form of a woman standing in the doorway. She appeared to be clad out-of-time, in a dress that reminded him of the mid-19th Century. She had a glowing, bluish hue that seemed to outline her body ... a body that was clearly missing its head.

He was transfixed for what seemed forever, yet couldn't have been more than a few seconds. In a move that implied haughty arrogance, she did what no headless being should be able to do: she caught up the hemline of her dress, wrapped it around herself, and floated past him, through the dining room of his home, and simply de-materialized.

He rushed to the kitchen window and peered out only to see the bluish translucence floating into the garden at Federal Hill.

To this day, no one has been able to come up with a satisfactory explanation as to why that one week in May 1974, could have been so supernaturally charged.[20]

How to Get There

From the Fredericksburg Visitor Center, take Charlotte Street west (uphill) to the 500 block.

Tips on Investigating

By all means, try the Crownover Technique, if you have the equipment, during daylight hours. Charlotte Street is not one of the busier streets in Fredericksburg, and so you may have luck with EVP. Try to get a name from the Lady in Blue so that further research can be done. Also, the street is public and open all night long. Be respectful of the property-owners' rights.

THE BATTLE OF CHANCELLORSVILLE

PRELUDE TO BATTLE

After the stunning Confederate victory at Fredericksburg in December 1862, Union General Ambrose E. Burnside attempted a winter march to flank Lee out of his position. Bogged down on the half-frozen, sloppy roads, it was dubbed "The Mud March," and signaled to those in Washington that Burnside was not the man to lead the Army of the Potomac.

Major General Joseph Hooker replaced Burnside in January 1863. Hooker, in addition to lending his name to the number of camp-followers who seemed to trail him and his troops wherever he went, also picked up, through a typographical error, the *nom de guerre* of "Fighting" Joe Hooker. As soon as he took command, he re-organized the army and came up with a plan for a spring offensive that appeared to be perfect.

He would send 10,000 cavalrymen on a sweep to cut Lee's communications with his capital, Richmond; part of Hooker's infantry would distract Lee with an attack upon Marye's Heights, while the bulk of it would march up the Rappahannock, cross, and fall on Lee's left and rear.

Lee had sent Longstreet and his troops south to gather supplies. He left himself with 60,000 men to face some 130,000 Federal troops. At the end of April, Hooker made his move, crossing Major General John Sedgwick's Sixth Corps at Fredericksburg to threaten Lee there and fording the Rappahannock upriver with 40,000 men. Lee, his army in a precarious trap, did what became his trademark: instead of retreating, he became aggressive.

By the afternoon of April 30, 1863, Hooker's main column, now numbering 50,000 and accompanied by 100 artillery pieces, broke out of the Wilderness and arrived at the Chancellorsville crossroads. But instead of pressing the advantage and securing all the lower fords across the river, much to the dismay of his subordinates, Hooker halted, waiting for more troops to arrive.

Thomas J. "Stonewall" Jackson, riding through the night of May 1, arrived on the battlefield and ordered the first Confederates he found to attack the Yankees. His aggressiveness forced Hooker to order his generals to fall back to a defensive position in the Wilderness. After planning a brilliant offensive, Hooker was intimidated into assuming a defensive role.

THE LAST BIVOUAC

That evening, a most momentous meeting took place. At the intersection of the Plank Road and Furnace Road, two of history's greatest commanders sat down on discarded cracker boxes and planned the perfect tactical battle. For Robert E. Lee it would lead to his most brilliant victory; for "Stonewall" Jackson, it would lead to his doom.

The Confederate cavalry commander, Major General J. E. B. Stuart had relayed the intelligence that Hooker's right flank was "in the air;" there were no natural obstacles—like a river—behind which the flank would be secure. Officers born and raised in the Wilderness area were consulted and a little-used road was located that would lead the Confederates directly to the Federals' flank. Sitting on his cracker-box, Jackson proposed to take his entire corps—nearly three-quarters of Lee's entire army—in a looping march along dusty wilderness roads, to strike the Federals in the flank. He would leave Lee with only 14,000 men to face Hooker's entire army. Lee thought for a moment, weighing the dangers if Hooker attacked while Jackson was marching, then gave Jackson orders to commence.

JACKSON'S FLANK MARCH

Early on the morning of May 2, Jackson's column snaked its way past the Lee-Jackson meeting site. Lee and Jackson spoke on horseback one more time. It was their last earthly meeting.

Reports of the movement reached Hooker. At first concerned that Lee might be headed toward his right flank, he then managed to convince himself that Lee was in retreat. He ordered Major General Daniel Sickles's Third Corps to attack what he thought was Lee's rear guard. The action drew more Union troops away from the main line, isolating the troops toward which Jackson's attack was aimed.

Jackson cemented Hooker's belief in his "retreat" by turning his column away from the enemy ... twice. Finally, by 3:00 P.M., after a twelve mile march, Jackson's men spread out into battle lines stretching a mile on either side of the Orange Turnpike. By 5:00 P.M., he was ready. Jackson's Corps faced only two unsuspecting Union regiments and a few cannon pointed in his direction.

JACKSON IS WOUNDED

On Hooker's extreme right flank, the men of the Federal 11th Corps were lounging, cooking meals, and relaxing with their weapons stacked. Suddenly, rabbits, deer, and other small game burst from the forest. Then from the darkening woods came the shrill call of bugles and the piercing rebel yell followed by sweat-soaked, wild-looking warriors charging into the Union campsites. Some Federals attempted to resist, but they were swept away. The 11th Corps disintegrated.

By 7:15 P.M. Jackson's attack ground to a halt. In spite of the darkness, Jackson intended to renew his attack as soon as he could re-organize in order to cut off the Federals from their retreat routes across the river. He called up Major General A. P. Hill's Division. As they were replacing the tired troops in the darkness, Jackson and his staff rode out in front of the lines to reconnoiter. Satisfied he had found the Federal line, he was returning when a skittish North Carolina regiment fired at what they thought was Yankee cavalry. It was Jackson's party. "Stonewall" took three bullets and was carried off the field. General A. P. Hill was also wounded, and J. E. B. Stuart was called from his cavalry duties to take command of Jackson's Corps. Realizing the difficulty in launching a night assault, he postponed Jackson's planned attack until the next day.

MAY 3—THE CONFEDERATE ATTACK CONTINUES

Knowing that Lee's army was still divided and in danger, Stuart devised a massive assault for dawn the next morning to re-connect the two wings. Hooker ordered Sickles to withdraw from the high ground at Hazel Grove to consolidate his lines. Stuart immediately captured Hazel Grove and placed 30 cannons there. At 5:30 A.M., May 3, Stuart began his attack down the Orange Plank Road. Brigade after brigade slammed into the Union lines until 9:30. The woods caught fire, and the wounded, unable to crawl away from the creeping flames, were cremated alive. The fighting in this area was some of the most intense of the American Civil War. In just a few square miles and in just five hours of combat, some 17,500 men became casualties.

During the fighting a Confederate shell struck one of the columns on the front of the Chancellor House where Union commander Hooker was standing. He was knocked senseless and, for all practical purposes, out of the rest of the battle. His final orders were clear, however: consolidate, fight defensively, and get the army back across the river as soon as practicable. The fight had gone out of "Fighting" Joe Hooker.

Stuart's column pushed forward simultaneously with Lee's wing which advanced from the south until Confederates swarmed around the Chancellorsville clearing. Just as Lee was about to drive the enemy into the river, word came from Fredericksburg that Sedgwick had done what Burnside couldn't and had driven the Confederates from Marye's Heights. He was now closing in on Lee's rear. Lee was forced to split his army once again, and send troops to stop the Yankees whom they met at Salem Church.

Fighting at Salem Church the next day, the rebels drove Sedgwick's men back across the Rappahannock River. Lee was then ready to turn to finishing off Hooker's army. But it was too late. Under the cover of darkness on May 5, the Union army withdrew across the Rappahannock, ending the fighting at Chancellorsville. The Federals lost 17,000 men as casualties during the battle. Although Lee lost 13,000, it was a higher percentage of his army. And, of course, the fighting at Chancellorsville cost the Confederate cause one of its greatest commanders, "Stonewall" Jackson. Complications from his wounds and amputation caused pneumonia to set in, and Jackson died on May 10, a loss from which the Confederacy would never recover.

Lee's incredible victory at Chancellorsville against overwhelming odds gave him confidence that his army was invincible. It was a false confidence that would be betrayed less than two months later ... at Gettysburg.

INVESTIGATING THE CHANCELLORSVILLE BATTLEFIELD

Paranormalists have catalogued numerous reasons why ghosts linger at one spot or another. At Gettysburg and Antietam they refer to the massive amounts of quartz-bearing granite rock as a possible source for "residual" hauntings—the type that seem to replay mindlessly, like a video or DVD, over and over. In Fredericksburg, the huge amount of energy available from the Rappahannock River is cited as perhaps the reason why there are so many sightings of spirit entities in the city.

Other paranormalists acknowledge that emotional energy can leave its supernatural mark nearly anywhere, regardless of the geology or energy sources. If that is so, Chancellorsville certainly qualifies as a source for incredible amounts of emotional energy.

The Confederacy, born as a dream for independence by a few of the southern states in 1860, was on the road to becoming a certainty by the time the armies reached Chancellorsville in May 1863. Outnumbered Confederate armies had, time and again, beaten better fed and better armed Yankees. Outside the gates of Washington, Confederates won their first major battle at Manassas; the next year they drove one of the largest Federal armies back from Richmond, down the James and York River Peninsula and, in that fighting, received a new commander, Robert E. Lee. They had seen Jackson's "foot cavalry" literally march circles around the Union armies in the Shennandoah Valley. Another battle near the old battleground of Manassas was a Confederate victory. They lost at Antietam, in September, 1862, but the Federals had failed to take advantage. Fredericksburg, in December, demonstrated how effective Lee's army could fight on the defensive. And now, this: perhaps the greatest offensive—certainly the most bittersweet—of all Confederate victories. Outnumbered, but never out-generalled, the Confederate Army of Northern Virginia after Chancellorsville was on an emotional high, rolling on to what would seem to be the securing of an independent nation in the southern half of what once was the "united" states.

Begin your investigation at the Chancellorsville Battlefield Visitor Center. From Fredericksburg, drive out Route 3 west approximately eleven miles. Watch for the brown and white National Park Service signs indicating the entrance to the Visitor Center on the right hand side. Explore the exhibits available in the building and around the grounds. As well, the National Park Service offers a large selection of books on the battle and the Civil War available for purchase in the Visitor Center.

BULLOCK HOUSE SITE

During the battle, the Bullock House became the apex of the final Union line at Chancellorsville. Intent on protecting their escape routes across the Rapidan and Rappahannock Rivers after Jackson's onslaught, the Federals formed a U-shaped battle line, studded with cannon, behind makeshift breastworks. As the interpretive plaques near the Bullock House Site indicate, Lee was ready to attack again on May 6, but Union commander Joseph Hooker had already retreated.

Bullock House Site

How to Get There
Leave the Chancellorsville Visitor Center parking lot. From the parking lot, follow the signs for the battlefield tour bearing right onto Bullock Road. The speed limit is 25 miles per hour. As you drive, note the Confederate trenches built by "Stonewall" Jackson's Corps about three-tenths of a mile from the Visitor Center on the right. The parking area for the Bullock House Site is on the right.

WARNING: An investigation after dark is not recommended due to the dangerous nature of the road. The National Park closes at dusk.

Tips on Investigating
The Bullock House Site is part of the Chancellorsville Battlefield administered by the National Park Service. The Bullock Road and the corner where the Bullock

House stood is closed at dusk. However, the Ely Ford Road is a public thoroughfare and open to the public at night. It is a well-traveled road.

The Bullock House Site, though, is somewhat off the road, so bring your recorder. A recent preliminary investigation with Investigative Medium Laine Crosby revealed how helpful having a "sensitive" with you on an investigation can be.

Remember, Laine had never been to Chancellorsville before, and had no idea where she was on the battlefield. Her first impression was that there was a "mix" of people in this area: a mix of "gray and blue" and a mix of people on foot and on horses. She felt, however, there were a lot more people on foot.

Before her was a broad open field, yet she said that she felt there may have been a house here, or a barn. Granted, she may have read the Park Service sign near the front of the parking area that said, "Bullock House Site," but she didn't know I was going to stop there. "There may have been a place where they piled a lot of bodies," she said. "There's an obstacle right there," she continued, pointing toward the house site.

We stopped in the field before we got to the Park Service interpretive signs. Laine commented that she felt, "a lot of confusion, a lot of things happened here. ... It's mixed together. That group back there, they have bayonets. That group came from back that way," she said, pointing towards the area where the Chancellorsville Visitor Center was located, the direction from which Jackson's attack came.

She pointed to the intersection of Ely Ford Road (Route 610) and Bullock Road, then over to Route 3. "Cannons!" she practically shouted. "Cannons ran through here." She paused. "They may have actually been sitting here, or pushed through here. There was more of a concentration of cannons here than out there," she said, pointing to the area of the Visitor Center. "I'm seeing mostly people running through there. The concentration of cannons seems behind me. The army came and, it was like, well, it's useless, because we could be shooting at our own men. So I don't think that they were fired, but not at the time that they were brought, if that makes any sense."

Historically, as far as her "seeing" (in her mind) the pile of bodies, according to Noel Harrison in his book *Chancellorsville Battlefield Sites*, between 1866 and 1868, 35 bodies of Federals soldiers were exhumed from the Bullock House area and taken to the National Cemetery in Fredericksburg. The "obstacle" she "saw" at the house can possibly be explained again by Harrison who quoted a Pennsylvania soldier: "At an angle in the breastworks lately constructed stood the White House."[1] As far as the confusion she felt, all battles have that. But at this particular juncture, the Union Army literally had its "brain" scrambled. General Hooker was lying in a tent at the Bullock House, trying to recover from being knocked senseless by a shell striking a column at the Chancellorsville Inn. The Pennsylvanian described the confusion, and sheds some light on Laine's comments about the cannons: "Officers were coming and going in hot, important haste, some with reports, others with directions. Guns [cannons] hurried to position were crashing to their places."[2] The final Union defensive line was quite formidable and formed a semi-circle bristling with cannons. The Pennsylvania soldier again may reveal what could possibly be an amazing coincidence, but may also be an incredible statement on a psychic's gift. He recalled what the area looked like in front of the breastworks and the Federal artillery:

"The open ground in front covered about one hundred and fifty yards, dipped slightly in the centre and terminated in a sparsely-wooded crest.

"In the timber on the crest was a Union line of battle, holding its regular formation, firing and loading with deliberation and slowly retiring."[3]

This would explain Laine's feelings about the cannons not being fired for fear of striking their own men.

She directed me to the edge of the clearing to attempt some EVP. The Ely Ford Road can be rather noisy, but with patience, you can pick up some EVP, as I did: In answer to my question, "Are you with the infantry?" I recorded a distinct, "Yes, Sir!"

As well, evening photos may yield a few of the misty spirits of the thousands of Union soldiers who once gathered at the road junction in order to save their army.

THE CHANCELLORSVILLE INN SITE

Chancellorsville Inn Site

"Chancellorsville" is actually a misnomer. The place never was a village, but rather a country wayside inn on the Plank Road.

The original house was built in 1816 as a tavern and inn for travelers past the intersection of Ely's Ford Road and Plank Road. During the 1863 battle, Frances Chancellor rented the property and lived there with her daughters operating the inn and tavern. By the afternoon of May 1, Union surgeons had turned the tidy tavern into a charnel house. Caring for the wounded continued through the night. The fourteen-year-old daughter of Frances Chancellor recalled in later years that their sitting room became an operating room and their piano the amputation table. The women were ordered into the basement which contained several inches of water, and were subjected to the screams and cries of the wounded above them through the night. The next day the house caught fire, and they were evacuated. On their way out they had a chance to glimpse the horrors of war that transformed their once lovely home into a grisly slaughter house: hideous pyramids of arms, legs, hands, and feet outside the windows of their sitting room; adjacent to the house, rows of corpses covered with canvas; the woods near the house afire; horses running, neighing in panic, and the men, cursing, praying, yelling, all in mass confusion. At least one doctor—Hichborn—was killed at the house on May 3.[4] Union Army commander Joseph Hooker was standing on the portico that morning when a solid shot struck one of the pillars, split it in two, and bowled over the general. He was knocked "senseless" for a while, recovered, but seemed to have lost his taste for battle: all his plans afterward involved the safe retreat of his army across the Rappahannock.[5]

The area around the house became a vast burial site: the bodies of 1,279 Union soldiers were removed from the vicinity of Chancellorsville during the great exhumation years of 1866–68.[6]

How to Get There

Leave the Chancellorsville Visitor Center parking lot. From the parking lot, follow the signs bearing right onto Bullock Road for the battlefield tour. From Bullock Road go to the stop sign at Ely's Ford Road and turn right. Follow the Park Service Battlefield Tour signs to stop #6, the Chancellorsville Inn site.

Tips on Investigating

The Chancellorsville Inn site is at a major intersection. EVP is probably not practical. An evening photographic investigation may yield results, but observe National Park Service regulations as to dusk restrictions on parking.

WARNING: Route 3 is a busy highway. Use caution when photographing, recording, or exploring near the road.

JACKSON'S AND LEE'S LAST BIVOUAC

If there ever was a Civil War site overflowing with lingering emotions, it would have to be the last bivouac site of Confederate Generals Robert E. Lee and Thomas J. "Stonewall" Jackson. The site represents the spot where they planned their most aggressive tactic of the war which would lead to Lee's greatest victory—the Battle of Chancellorsville—as well as his greatest loss: the wounding of Jackson in the subsequent action. The site also represents the place where Jackson would spend his last night on an earthly battlefield.

Around dusk, Lee and Jackson met at the junction of the Plank Road and Furnace Road. Harassed by Yankee sharpshooters, they moved to the northwest corner of the junction, sat down together and discussed the battle and their options. An attack upon Hooker's right flank was one of those. It was then that J. E. B. Stuart arrived with the news that Hooker's right flank was "in the air." Lee and Jackson discussed some details then retired for the night, curled up on the damp ground.

Jackson's and Lee's Last Bivouac Site

It was one of those strange occurrences that men, upon retrospect, take as omens of a divine will that cannot be denied. Before he lay down to sleep, Jackson unbuckled his sword and leaned it up against a nearby tree. The brief night on the ground in the woods was cool with the early May dampness. Some historians say that ill-advised slumber in the dew added to Jackson's already lingering bronchial distress; when he was wounded and weakened from his amputation, historians point to this night on the cold ground as a factor in the pneumonia which eventually killed him. One of Lee's aides, Colonel Armistead Long awoke before dawn on May 2 to see Jackson warming his hands by a small fire. He brought Jackson a cup of coffee and sat to talk. Suddenly, there was a clatter of metal from the darkness. Jackson's sword, so carefully placed against the tree just a couple of hours before, with no human hand touching it, crashed to the ground. Apprehensively, Long picked it up and handed it to Jackson. Neither man, at the moment, said anything about it, but Long remembered it many years after the war, and knowing what he knew then of Jackson's impending fate, considered it a harbinger of ill. A commanders' sword falling to the ground untouched, pushed perhaps, by the unseen forces swirling about a legendary Confederate officer who, had he lived, may have changed the course of American history. . . .

How to Get There

From the Chancellorsville Visitor Center, continue to follow the Battlefield Tour across Route 3, to stop # 7, the Lee-Jackson Bivouac Site. Turn right on Furnace Road and park in the designated area.

Tips on Investigating

While their last conference would seem fairly businesslike at the time, the last meeting of Robert E. Lee and his loved and trusted subordinate Thomas J. "Stonewall" Jackson, increases in significance in retrospect. What they planned at this little crossroads was nothing less than one of the most studied battle tactic in all of military history. Young officers and wizened generals have pondered for nearly a century-and-a-half what they would have done had they been in the same situation: Divide your army for a third time in the face of the enemy and risk a flank march; or play it safe and retreat to fight another day?

Once again, Laine Crosby, during a preliminary field investigation in July, 2007, showed how astounding some mediums can be. She had never visited Chancellorsville before, had never been to the Lee/Jackson bivouac site, yet came up with information that could not be in her realm of conscious knowledge.

Almost as soon as we left the car she asked if there was a dirt road here at the time of the battle. It may be true that any road in the area would have been dirt, or "plank," meaning half covered with wooden beams. But the National Park Service is known to have installed modern roads where there were no historical roads for visitors to access battle sites, so her intuition made sense: She felt that this was one of the original roads, and, in fact, the Furnace Road was. She asked if a wealthy family had lived nearby, because she "saw" (in her mind) a lot of girls, giggling and moving as if they were going to a party. I was fairly certain that no one could prove whether there had been a party in the vicinity . . . until I re-read the segment of Noel Harrison's book, *Chancellorsville Battlefield Sites* and realized that on December 10, 1862, some of J. E. B. Stuart's staff went to a party that Harrison was pretty sure occurred at the Alrich House, formerly located near the junction of the Plank Road and Catharpin Road, only a mile southeast of where we stood. It was customary for Stuart and his staff to attend balls or galas and invite all the young women in the area.

Laine suddenly said, "I'm feeling a lot of people, a lot of energy coming this way." She gestured from the intersection of the Plank Road and Furnace Road towards herself. "And they're not fighting," she continued. "They're coming to fight . . . they're going somewhere else to fight. I'm not getting fighting here. A large number of men, not hundreds, but thousands. They're on horses and on foot. They're mixed." We had not yet reached the Lee/Jackson bivouac site and were standing in the middle of the Furnace Road, in the very space through which

"Stonewall" Jackson's men marched some fourteen decades before. She described exactly what Jackson's men were doing: marching on a twelve-mile flanking maneuver to do their fighting somewhere else. The number of men with Jackson: some 12,000. Laine also described exactly how a column of infantry and their officers would have looked traveling on this road.

The area is not well traveled and may lend itself to obtaining EVP. If you feel uncomfortable attempting to contact Robert E. Lee or "Stonewall" Jackson, try some of their aides who were there: Jackson's chaplain, Tucker Lacy; Jackson's aides Alexander "Sandie" Pendleton and James Power Smith; Lee's aide Colonel Armistead Long; Jackson's engineer and map-maker Jedediah Hotchkiss.

Sometimes subordinate officers will answer attempts at EVP. I was on an investigation at Union Mills, Maryland, where J. E. B. Stuart encamped a couple of nights before the Battle of Gettysburg. I was attempting to get EVP in a quiet back room. Even though I wrote a book about him, I certainly wasn't presumptuous enough to believe I would be able to contact Major General Stuart himself. Instead, I had done some research and discovered that one of Stuart's aides was Major Andrew Reid Venable. I chose to address him.

Armed with my Panasonic RR-DR60 IC digital recorder set on "voice activation," I began to ask some questions of the young officer. Of course, after asking the questions, there was complete silence in the room. There was no sound—nothing—to indicate that anything was being recorded. Nothing except the steadily glowing light and advancing numbers on the recorder! When I hit the playback button, we were astounded at what we heard:

Mark: "Major Venable, did you ride in with General Stuart?"
Answer: "I did."
Mark: Major Venable, who is president?"
Answer: "J ... Je ... Jefferson Davis."
We had made contact in intelligent conversation with the Other World!

There is a slight trail back into the woods from the northwest corner. An investigation with cameras either in the daylight, using the Crownover Technique for photographing spirit energies in the daylight, or near infrared ("Night-shot") near dusk could yield some interesting results. Once again, obey National Park regulations and avoid parking after dark.

Hazel Grove

Hazel Grove actually refers to a homestead, owned by the Chancellor family, located upon one of the higher ridges about a mile southwest of Chancellorsville. The only high ground suitable for artillery use, the area became hotly contested during the fighting.

The Federal Army's Third Corps occupied the area as Hooker filled in his line in an advanced position between Slocum's 12th Corps and Howard's 11th Corps. The Third Corps was commanded by Major General Daniel Sickles, a "political" general who had no formal military training, yet wielded enough clout in his native New York to recruit an entire brigade—the "Excelsior Brigade"—and rise in the ranks from there. Sickles was convinced from what he saw that part of Lee's army was on the moved westward—either in retreat or getting into position to flank Hooker's army.[7] Sickles requested that he be allowed to attack. Leading the attack was an elite unit, Berdan's Sharpshooters. They picked a fight with some of Jackson's moving column. Lee sent in a brigade to help; Sickles sent in more troops and a general firefight ensued, but did not impede Jackson's march.

Hazel Grove

Sickles sent for some cavalry to back him up. Brigadier General Alfred Pleasonton arrived with three regiments and horse artillery. Soon afterward there came an unsettling report that "Stonewall" Jackson's men—that column of troops many Union officers thought was retreating—had turned in a sharp arc. They had lined up in battle formation, and were attacking Howard's 11th Corps, the right of the entire Union Army. Pleasonton ordered the 8th Pennsylvania Cavalry, resting their horses at the north edge of the clearing at Hazel Grove, to help out Howard. Major Pennock Huey led the regiment, followed by Major Peter Keenan, who was pulled away from a poker game he was apparently winning. It seems that from that moment, Keenan's Irish luck had truly run dry.

In the woods they ran into Jackson's flankers on both sides of their column. There was only one thing to do. Huey called to his men to draw sabers and charge. They attacked toward the Plank Road, then turned left and ran smack into the main body of Confederates. They managed to drive a hundred yards into the attacking mass before the surprised Confederates organized and fired devastating volleys into the packed horsemen. One third of the leading troopers went down, including Captain Charles Arrowsmith, Adjutant J. Haseltine Haddock, and Major Keenan. When they found his body, Keenan had been perforated by thirteen minie balls.[8]

A story comes down from a park ranger relating the experience of another ranger who was at Hazel Grove. It was evening. He had exited his car and was walking among the cannons placed there to illustrate the positions where Confederate artillery once stood and dealt their deadly projectiles. The shadows began to gather and play tricks upon the eyes. That… in the distance… is that a horse? Or several? No. Couldn't be. The senses can be fooled so easily, especially in near darkness, and especially on a battlefield where so many struggled and died. Just then, from a completely calm night, a strong breeze rushed past him, strong enough to rustle the leaves on nearby trees. But rustling leaves was not the only thing he heard that eerie night. From somewhere within that rushing, localized wind, came the sound of scores of pounding horses' hooves, galloping rhythmically, so near he could almost hear the squeak of the stirrup leathers and clank of sabers. Then, as quickly as it came, the sound vanished into the timeless, formless darkness, and the strange wind that seemed to transport the audible impossibility, fell once again into a deathlike stillness.

How to Get There

From the Lee-Jackson Bivouac Site, follow Furnace Road to Sickles Drive and turn right. Pass Slocum Drive and Berry-Paxton Drive on your right. Park in the designated area for Hazel Grove and walk to the interpretive plaques and cannon.

Tips on Investigating

Attempts at obtaining EVP on two separate occasions yielded some interesting results. On March 4, 2006, I was part of an investigation at Hazel Grove and was asked to try to get some EVP. I was standing in the woods near the parking area and addressed various officers and men of the Confederacy. The results were positive: I was receiving background "white" noise as well as what sounded like answers to some questions. Some unusual sounds I received were clicks, like someone snapping their fingers. I asked, "Are you Federal or Rebel?" and got a garbled answer. I praised the men for their valor and thanked them for their help.

A second visit to Hazel Grove was a little more rewarding. On July 2, 2007 (coincidentally the anniversary of the second day at Gettysburg), I tried contacting Major Keenan and Major Huey. Only one appeared to respond. After asking for Major Huey, a rhythmic clopping sound, like horses' hooves was heard, then a muffled, three-beat sentence. Hazel Grove is a site worth attempting EVP.

FAIRVIEW

For much of the Battle of Chancellorsville, the Fairview farmstead was a Union artillery position. Union General Alpheus Williams had his headquarters there on

April 30. The house at Fairview was made of wood (at least two individuals depicted it as "log") and, though "dilapidated," without doors or windows, suffered hits from Confederate artillery at Hazel Grove on May 1. The building was about thirty feet long and twenty feet wide with three or four rooms. Surgeons used the building to house the seriously wounded and perhaps performed operations there. On May 2, thirty-four Union cannon stretched in an artillery line along the west side of Fairview. (Gun pits from their original position, facing south, can still be seen.) Cannons from near this position were involved in firing at the party attempting to carry the wounded "Stonewall" Jackson from the battlefield on the evening of May 2. For three hours on the morning of May 3, these guns doggedly defended the position against J. E. B. Stuart's assault. But by 9:00 a.m., with ammunition running dangerously low, the guns were withdrawn. A Federal soldier examining the area of Fairview after the battle noticed dozens of dead Confederates lying in front of the gunners' position, all riddled by canister, the shells filled with lead and iron balls, used by artillery like giant shotgun shells against packed infantry. Just as disgustingly grotesque were the bodies of hundreds of horses, carcasses bloated, legs pointed to the sky.

Courtesy of Kathleen Butcher

Fairview

As the Union artillery abandoned the position, Confederate artillery from Hazel Grove advanced and took it up, lobbing shells at the Chancellorsville headquarters of General Hooker. The shells fired from Fairview ignited the inn and dismantled the pillar which struck and disabled the Union Commander. By the end of the battle, Robert E. Lee had pitched his headquarters tents here, ready to renew the fight, only to learn that Hooker had withdrawn across the river.

Around the broken-down log cabin lay some five hundred Union wounded being cared for by Confederate and captured Union surgeons.

How to Get There
From Hazel Grove, you may take a self-guided walking tour across the fields to Fairview. Along the way there are several tour stops. Or, from Hazel Grove, return along Stuart Drive and turn left on Berry-Paxton Drive. The National Park Service provides a parking area near Fairview.

Tips on Investigating
Though the house is no longer standing, a photographic or videographic investigation in that area might reveal some residual energies. With so many wounded having been brought to the area around the Fairview log cabin, there may still be residual spirit energy haunting the area. An appeal to wounded Union soldiers still in the area may yield results. The area in front of the artillery line (about where Walking Tour Stop # 5 is marked), was the place where the Union soldier witnessed the scores of Confederates ripped apart by canister. It may also hold the remnants of anguished Southerners, killed in a battle that, while a major victory, would still not win the war.

The trail that leads to Fairview is almost in the center of National Park property and is relatively unused, so it's quiet. The walking trail to Fairview would be the ideal place to try recording EVP. If you drive to the site, you may be able to remain a little closer to dusk and attempt infrared photography of remnant spirit energy. Using the Crownover Technique, you can try to photograph the energies any time of day.

SALEM CHURCH

Built in 1844, the Baptist Church became a refuge for citizens of Fredericksburg fleeing the fighting in their town in November and December, 1862. On May 3, 1863, it became a whirlpool of battle.

Confederate infantry formed a line across the Plank Road just west of the church, ensconced in ready-made earthworks built as a reserve position by Confederates during the 1862 battle of Fredericksburg. Around 5:00 p.m. Union artillery farther east on the Plank Road opened on them. Shortly after, Union infantry stretched out on either side of the road, advanced and clashed with the entrenched Confederates. Four Confederate sharpshooters took up positions in the pulpit of the church and fired out the eastern windows.[9] The Union line fought its way right up to the churchyard. An Alabaman captain recalled that the Yankees were firing from one end of the building and the Confederates from the other. As the Yankees began to retreat from the withering fire, Colonel Mark Collet of the 1st New Jersey was shot dead as he tried to slow the withdrawal. At the end of the battle, a witness saw parallel lines of dead men at either end of the church.[10]

Salem Church

The fighting had barely died down when Confederate surgeons took over the building and turned it from church to charnel house. One of the surgeons working there was George R. C. Todd, brother of Mary Todd Lincoln, President Abraham Lincoln's wife. Colonel Robert McMillan remembered the horror inside the little country church: "The amputated limbs were piled up in every corner almost as high as a man could reach; blood flowed in streams along the aisles and out the doors…"

Some ninety-two Union soldiers and an unknown number of Confederates were buried around the building.[11]

How to Get There

From the Chancellorsville Visitor Center follow Route 3 east about 6 miles to Salem Church Road and turn right. Follow the signs to Old Salem Church and park in the lot.

WARNING: The area is owned by the National Park Service and is governed by the visitation restrictions: please leave the area by dusk.

Tips for Investigating

Previous paranormal investigations have yielded still photos of what appear to be paranormal energies around the church. Beware of false positives from reflections in the windows. There is obviously activity around the old church. You may have to take photographs near dusk or use the Crownover Technique to attempt to capture spirit entities during the daylight hours.

Because noisy Route 3 is so close to the church, attempts at EVP are not recommended.

ENDNOTES

Introduction

[1] Books like *The Holographic Universe*, by Michael Talbot (HarperCollins, 1991) and *The Physics of Immortality*, by Frank J. Tipler (Doubleday, 1994) and additional research published abroad have drawn the paranormal and the science of physics closer than ever before.

[2] Francis A. O'Reilly, *The Fredericksburg Campaign: Winter War on the Rappahannock* (Baton Rouge: LSU Press, 2003), 446. This is one of the finest books I have read on the Battle of Fredericksburg and recommend it highly to novice and serious students alike.

[3] Ibid., 458-461.

The Battle of Fredericksburg

[1] O'Reilly, 139-140.

[2] National Park Service, "Fredericksburg Battlefields" Official National Park Handbook # 155, (Washington, D. C.: U. S. Department of the Interior), 29.

[3] H. B. McClellan, *I Rode with Jeb Stuart: The Life and Campaigns of Maj. Gen J. E. B. Stuart*, (Burke Davis, ed., Bloomington, IN: Indiana University Press, 1958),195.

[4] A number of Civil War battlefields have their "Slaughter Pens," but the one at Fredericksburg seems huge, covering several acres. Gettysburg's "Slaughter Pen," near Devil's Den, in contrast, can be seen in a glance.

[5] O'Reilly, 252.

[6] Ibid., 257.

[7] Ibid., 326.

[8] Ibid., 308.

[9] Ibid., 312.

[10] Ibid., 346.

Investigating the Fredericksburg Battlefield

[1] Noel G. Harrison, *Fredericksburg Civil War Sites, December 1862-April 1865*. Volume Two. (Lynchburg, VA: H. E. Howard, Inc.: 1995), 226-227.

[2] O'Reilly. 89-94.

[3] O'Reilly, 264.

4 Harrison, Vol. 2, 179-180.

5 O'Reilly, 308.

6 Harrison, Vol. 2, 175.

7 Brigadier General John W. Ames, quoted in Mark Nesbitt, *Through Blood and Fire: Selected Civil War Papers of Major General Joshua Chamberlain* (Mechanicsburg, PA: Stackpole Books, 1996), 41.

8 Teri A. Jeske, "Martha Stephens: The Woman Behind the Legend," *The Journal of Fredericksburg History,* Vol. 2. (Fredericksburg VA: Historic Fredericksburg Foundation, 1997). For more on Martha Stephens, see also, Donald C. Pfanz, *War So Terrible: A Popular History of the Battle of Fredericksburg,* (Richmond: Page One History Publications, 2003), "Martha Stephens: Heroine or Hoax?" 85-87.

9 Harrison, Vol. 2, 127-131.

10 Pfanz, *War So Terrible*, "The Struggle for Prospect Hill", 60-62.

11 Ibid., 191.

12 Donald C. Pfanz, "American Golgotha: The Creation and Early History of Fredericksburg National Cemetery," *The Journal of Fredericksburg History,* Vol. 9. (Fredericksburg, VA: Historic Fredericksburg Foundation, 2005), 9-12.

13 According to maps in Frank O'Reilly's *The Fredericksburg Campaign* (329 & 395), the Pennsylvania regiments which assaulted across this area in an attempt to take the Sunken Road included the 53rd, 127th, 72nd, 106th, 69th, 155th, 133rd, 123rd, 131st, 129th, 134th, 91st, and 126th.

14 Emily Battle, "Remains Discovered at Maury work site." (Fredericksburg, VA: *The Free Lance-Star*), week of Feb. 19, 2007.

15 Harrison, *Fredericksburg civil War Sites*, Vol. II, 194.

16 The "alerting" of animals is an important, but of ten overlooked detecting device in paranormal studies. Humans enter a paranormal situation with "baggage," and will often talk themselves out of believing what they have just experienced. "It was something under my contact lens," or "It must have been my imagination," is what many people use to rationalize away a paranormal event. Animals have no such rationalizations. Dogs just "alert" to what they see, hear or smell, i.e. to what is real, proving that paranormal activity is not a figment of one's imagination.

17 Harrison, Vol. 2, 147-149.

18 Ibid., 241-244.

19 "Remote Viewing" is when a sensitive travels to a place in her mind and sees various aspects of the site. The sensitive is able to view the place from different angles and in different time periods. Strange as this may sound, the U. S. Military had a training program for remote viewers from 1972 to 1995 named Project STARGATE which was conducted at Fort Meade in Maryland.

20 L. B. Taylor, Jr., "The Headless Blue Lady of Charlotte Street," *The Ghosts of Fredericksburg*, 66-69. L. B. Taylor, as I have called him before, is the dean of Virginia ghost stories having numerous volumes to his name.

Investigating the Chancellorsville Battlefield

1   Noel G. Harrison, *Chancellorsville Battlefield Sites*, 2nd Edition, (Lynchburg, VA: H. E. Howard, Inc., 1990), 13.

2   Ibid., 14.

3   Ibid., 14.

4   Ibid., 16-20.

5   There are several fine books out on the Chancellorsville Campaign; all agree that after conceptualizing and pulling off a fine offensive maneuver, Hooker suddenly lost his nerve and began thinking not only defensively, but how to withdraw his army out of the field of conflict. Being knocked unconscious at the Chancellor House seemed to merely hasten Hooker's plans to retreat.

6   Harrison, *Chancellorsville Battlefield Sites*, 20.

7   Ernest B. Furgurson, *Chancellorsville, 1863: The Souls of the Brave*. (New York: Vintage Books, 1993), 147-154.

8   Ibid., 188.

9   Ibid., 274-279.

10 Harrison, *Chancellorsville Battlefield Sites*, 161-163.

11 USNPS Interpretive sign at Salem Church.

RESOURCES

Paranormal Equipment:
Edmund Scientifics
800-728-6999
www.scientificsonline.com

Less EMF Inc.
518-432-1550
www.lessemf.com

Internet Sites:
American Association for Electronic Voice Phenomena (AA-EVP)
PO Box 13111
Reno, Nevada 89507
www.aaevp.com

Instrumental Transcommunication—Ghost voices over the telephone; communication
via fax and computer, and pictures of the dead appearing on television screens
www.worlditc.org

Broad information on the paranormal from a lawyer who de-bunks the de-bunkers:
www.victorzammit.com

Unique programming combining historical documentary with paranormal reality
and adventure:
www.ghostchannel.tv

Troy Taylor's expansive web site with many stories and links:
www.prairieghosts.com

Investigative Medium Laine Crosby
www.investigativemedium.com
www.ghostchannel.tv

Clearing house for all things pertaining to the paranormal:
www.HauntedAmericaTours.com

Books Relating to Ghosts:

Nesbitt, Mark. *The Ghost Hunter's Field Guide: Gettysburg and Beyond*. Gettysburg: Second Chance Publications, 2005.

Nesbitt, Mark. *Ghosts of Gettysburg*. Gettysburg: Thomas Publications, 1991.

_____. *More Ghosts of Gettysburg*. Gettysburg: Thomas Publications, 1992.

_____. *Ghosts of Gettysburg III*. Gettysburg: Thomas Publications, 1995.

_____. *Ghosts of Gettysburg IV*. Gettysburg: Thomas Publications, 1998.

_____. *Ghosts of Gettysburg V*. Gettysburg: Thomas Publications, 2000.

_____. *Ghosts of Gettysburg VI*. Gettysburg: Second Chance Publications, 2004.

Solomon, Grant & Jane. *The Scole Experiment: Scientific Evidence for Life After Death*. Piatkus Books, 1999. The true story of a group of experimenters connecting with a "team" of scientists from the afterlife to exchange information.

Schwartz, Dr. Gary. *The Afterlife Experiments : Breakthrough Scientific Evidence of Life After Death*. New York: Atria, *2002*. A scientist's experiments on communicating with the dead.

Taylor, Troy. *The Ghost Hunters Guidebook: The Essential Handbook for Ghost Research*. Alton, IL: Whitechapel Productions Press, 2001. Great tips and techniques.

Warren, Joshua P. *How to Hunt Ghosts: A Practical Guide*. New York: Simon & Schuster, 2003. More good information on paranormal investigations.

History of Fredericksburg:

O'Reilly, Francis A. *The Fredericksburg Campaign: Winter War on the Rappahannock* (Baton Rouge: LSU Press, 2003). This is one of the most comprehensive, yet readable books ever written on the Battle of Fredericksburg. It is recommended highly to novice and serious student alike.

National Park Service, "Fredericksburg Battlefields" Official National Park Handbook # 155, (Washington, D. C.: U. S. Department of the Interior).

Harrison, Noel G. *Fredericksburg Civil War Sites*, December 1862-April 1865. Volumes 1 & 2. (Lynchburg, VA: H. E. Howard, Inc.: 1995).

Pfanz, Donald C. *War So Terrible: A Popular History of the Battle of Fredericksburg*, (Richmond: Page One History Publications, 2003).

Taylor, L. B., Jr. *The Ghosts of Fredericksburg*. L. B. Taylor has written over a dozen volumes of ghost stories of Virginia, including the popular, Ghosts of Williamsburg, and Civil War Ghosts of Virginia. If you love ghost stories, read L. B. Taylor.

History of Chancellorsville:

Harrison, Noel G. *Chancellorsville Battlefield Sites*, 2nd Edition, (Lynchburg, VA: H. E. Howard, Inc., 1990).

Furgurson, Ernest B. *Chancellorsville, 1863: The Souls of the Brave*. (New York: Vintage Books, 1993).

The *Time-Life* Series, "The Civil War," *Rebels Resurgent: Fredericksburg to Chancellorsville*.

"... scientific study and reflection had taught us that the known universe of three dimensions embraces the merest fraction of the whole cosmos of substance and energy."

H. P. Lovecraft

GHOST INVESTIGATION CHECKLIST

Location:

Investigator(s):

Brief History of Site (Include names of historical individuals associated with the site. If a building is involved, include interviews with owners or residents regarding paranormal events):

Date:

Time: Start_____Finish_____

Weather: Rain____Fog____Snow____Clear_____

Temperature:

Humidity: Dry___ Damp___

Moon Phase:

Sunset/Sunrise Time:

Solar Activity:

Equipment & Methods Used:

Video (Type):_____Night shot used?_____

Cameras (Digital or other type):_____

Audio (Digital or magnetic tape):_____

Remote Temperature Meter (Thermal Scanner):_____

EMF Meter: _____

Results: (See also attachments with photos)

Time:_____Event:

Time:_____Event:

Time:_____Event:

Time:_____Event:

Time:_____Event:

GHOST INVESTIGATION CHECKLIST

Location:

Investigator(s):

Brief History of Site (Include names of historical individuals associated with the site. If a building is involved, include interviews with owners or residents regarding paranormal events):

Date:
Time: Start_____Finish_____
Weather: Rain____Fog____Snow____Clear_____
Temperature:
Humidity: Dry___ Damp___
Moon Phase:
Sunset/Sunrise Time:
Solar Activity:

Equipment & Methods Used:
Video (Type):_____Night shot used?_____
Cameras (Digital or other type):_____
Audio (Digital or magnetic tape):_____
Remote Temperature Meter (Thermal Scanner):_____
EMF Meter: _____
Results: (See also attachments with photos)

Time:_____**Event:**

Time:_____**Event:**

Time:_____**Event:**

Time:_____**Event:**

Time:_____**Event:**

Mark Nesbitt was born in Lorain, Ohio, and graduated from Baldwin-Wallace College with a BA in English Literature. He worked for the National Park Service in Gettysburg, Pennsylvania, as a Ranger/Historian for five years and then became a Licensed Battlefield Guide. He started his own research and writing company in 1977.

Mr. Nesbitt has been a keynote speaker and guest lecturer for numerous colleges and universities, political, civic, and trade associations. He has won several awards and has been seen or heard on The History Channel, A&E, The Discovery Channel, The Travel Channel, Unsolved Mysteries, Coast to Coast AM, on regional television and radio programs, as well as, local newspapers. His *Ghosts of Gettysburg Candlelight Walking Tour*° was named the #1 ghost tour in the country by the readers of HauntedAmericaTours.com in 2007 and 2008.

In 2006, Mr. Nesbitt started the Ghosts of Fredericksburg Tours in Fredericksburg, Virginia.

Other books by Mark Nesbitt:

Ghosts of Gettysburg
More Ghosts of Gettysburg
Ghosts of Gettysburg III
Ghosts of Gettysburg IV
Ghosts of Gettysburg V
Ghosts of Gettysburg VI

The Ghost Hunter's Field Guide: Gettysburg & Beyond

Haunted Pennsylvania

If the South Won Gettysburg

35 Days to Gettysburg: The Campaign Diaries of Two American Enemies

Rebel Rivers: A Guide to Civil War Sites on the Potomac, Rappahannock, York, and James

Saber and Scapegoat: J.E.B. Stuart and the Gettysburg Controversy

Through Blood and Fire: The Selected Civil War Papers of Major General Joshua Chamberlain

Sixty Things to Do When You Turn Sixty (contributing author).

To order any of Mark Nesbitt's books please visit:

www.ghostsofgettysburg.com

Or write to:

Second Chance Publications
P. O. Box 3126
Gettysburg, PA 17325
info@secondchancepublications.com

Mark Nesbitt's
Ghosts of Gettysburg Candlelight Walking Tours

Gettysburg may very well be,
acre for acre,
the most haunted place in America.

Over the years since the infamous battle, stories of scores of sightings, stranger than reality, have emerged from the quaint houses and gentle fields in and around the town of Gettysburg: Stories of sightings of soldiers, moving again in battle lines, across the fields where they once marched ... and died; tales of visions through a rip in time into the horrible scene of a Civil War hospital; whispers of a look at men long dead held eternally captive by duty. These apparitions—and more—come back to remind us, in one way or another that they are not to be forgotten for what they did here ...

In 1994, Mark Nesbitt started the first ghost walk in Gettysburg. Armed with tales from his ghost books—and with a few that are not in the books—guides dressed in period attire take visitors on evening tours through sections of town that were bloody battlefields 13 decades ago; through night-darkened streets to houses and buildings where it is not as quiet as it should be; to sites on the old Pennsylvania College campus where the slain once lay in rows, and the wounded suffered horribly, waiting to become corpses themselves; to cemeteries where the dead lie ... sometimes not so peacefully.

For more information on *The Ghosts of Gettysburg Candlelight Walking Tours*, please visit our web site:

www.ghostsofgettysburg.com

Or write to:
Ghosts of Gettysburg
271 Baltimore Street
Gettysburg, PA 17325

Or call/fax/email:
717.337.0445
fx: 717.337.9673
hauntgburg@aol.com

Mark Nesbitt's
Ghosts of Fredericksburg Tours

Fredericksburg, Virginia:
the most haunted city,
per capita,
in the entire United States.

From a past that stretches back to pre-Colonial times, to the horror of being the focal point of four major Civil War battles that claimed over 100,000 casualties.

Combining history with mysterious tales of the still lurking dead, costumed guides conduct 80 minute, comfortably-paced, candlelight walking tours through sections of town that have seen and heard the spirit remnants from the 18th Century of a phantom harpist and singer and of the frustrated lover who still strolls along what locals have named the "Ghost Walk" once every seven years; tours walk down darkened Caroline Street and hear stories of long dead Fredericksburg residents who still inhabit the many historic buildings; they see the modern restaurant in an historic home where a woman allegedly hanged herself in shame after being exposed as a Yankee collaborator; they return past the church where the apparitional "Woman in White" was first seen in 1858, and again just a year ago.

Join us for the most unique tour available in night-time Fredericksburg.

For more information on *The Ghosts of Fredericksburg Tours*, please visit our web site:

www.ghostsoffredericksburg.com

Or write to:
Ghosts of Fredericksburg
P.O. Box 121
Fredericksburg, VA 22404

Or call/fax/email:
540.654.5414
fx: 540.654.5415
info@ghostsoffredericksburg.com

TRAVEL through parts of the battlefield where no other ghost tours go...

SEE haunted Oak Ridge, where the phantom messenger still rides and the wails of the dying have been heard...fourteen decades after their deaths...

RIDE past the modern engine house, as seen on the Travel Channel's Mysterious Journeys...next to the bloody railroad cut...

HEAR electronic voice phenomena (EVP)—believed to be the mutterings of the dead recorded on tape at the engine house—as well as some of the most frightening stories of ghost trains in American Folklore, such as:

- » *The Christmas Train Disaster and the hauntings it spawned.*
- » *The Zouave who still searches a railroad cut for something missing since the Battle of Second Manassas.*
- » *The ghosts of soldiers who survived Gettysburg, then died horribly in a train wreck.*
- » *The lights still seen of a mournful train carrying wounded soldiers... from the Civil War.*
- » *The most famous ghost train, carrying a slain president, still seen to this day.*

Please allow at least 2 hours for the ride.

For more information or reservations:

www.gettysburgrail.com

Pioneer Lines Scenic Railway
106 N. Washington Street
Gettysburg, PA 17325
717.334.6932
pioneerlines@innernet.net